The Impo~~rtance~~

of

Being Average

Existing as a Nobody in the Age of Somebody

A Manual on Appreciating Under-Achievement

by John Grace, M.D.
(A very average doctor)

John Grace

The Importance of Being Average

You can be special to a few people some of the time.

You can be special to no one all of the time.

But you can be average to most people most of the time.

Be average.

John Grace

The Importance of Being Average

Join the Average Revolution

(Just don't be too enthusiastic about it.)

www.beingaverage.com

John Grace

Introduction

One comment people say when they first see this book is, "But John, you *aren't* average. You're a doctor. You've written a book. How can you call yourself average?"

Average is not an absolute, it's not a *reality*—it's a *mentality*. Average is about your relationship with yourself. Average is about the human mind.

The other day I was driving to the *University of South Florida* to give a lecture to physicians in training. It had been a crazy week with Halloween, three birthday parties, a move to a new office, a new employee, and another lecture to the *National Alliance for the Mentally Ill*.

The title of my lecture?

"Keeping balance in your life."

Yeah right. Practicing what you preach isn't easy. I've helped a lot of over achievers through the years...myself included. This book has helped a lot of them...myself included. But even though they're the ones who need this book the most, they're the ones *least* likely to buy into it...myself included.

I never thought much of average, never tried to find it, until I understood the reasoning behind it, the science behind average. I'm a *"facts-first"* kind of guy. So if you're like me, if you're one of those people that *needs* science up front, if everyone says you work too hard but you *know* they're wrong, you *know* you're lazy, if a humorous little book couldn't possibly have anything profound to say about the human mind, then go ahead and turn to Appendix A. Read *The Science of Average*. You'll find all the sociology, psychology, and evolutionary biology

John Grace

you require to start reading this book. If you absolutely *need* that to be open to a new idea then by all means go there but for the rest of you...sit back and find average the way it was meant to be found—through laughter.

CONTENTS

PART I
"FINDING AVERAGE"

PART II
"SAVING AVERAGE"

PART III
"BEING AVERAGE"

PART I

FINDING AVERAGE

For Pete's sake, don't think of this book as changing your life! It never will if you do.

Just because a situation has dramatic consequences, doesn't mean that drama is the most appropriate approach. Think of this book with less intense emotion but more consistent emotion. Try to let it change you in the slightest way but change you forever. In the long run, that change means more.

You should never read it with a lot of focus but you should read it many times. Have a humorous, nonchalant approach to it.

If you *tell* anyone to read it, you're missing the point. If you suggest it to more than two people, you're missing the point. This little book doesn't want to part of any big discussions or change. It doesn't want to be on a book club reading list. There shouldn't be any expletives tied to your description of it. It shouldn't be the best or worst thing that anyone has read.

It's an amusing little curiosity that a few people can chuckle at. Keep it that way.

Do not keep this book in good repair. There should be several frayed edges with worn pages—maybe a coffee stain or two. It should get discolored over time and euthanized in its day or perhaps sold for a quarter at your garage sale.

But give it a little respect. It is a book after all. Let it stick around your house for a while. It's not a newspaper for goodness sake. It isn't a flyer. Give it some dignity. It's better than your junk mail, catalogues, and coupons. It should have more of a shelf life than the *Sunday Times*, but doesn't belong next to the family photo albums—except for on my mom's shelf.

You shouldn't mark any of the pages or memorize any of the sentences verbatim. But you are allowed to recall some general ideas to drop as your own at the water cooler. You can even daydream about some of the themes from time to time.

It can be a bathroom book. That's where most average books hang out. That's where good magazines end up. I think this book would be very happy as a bathroom book. Let it live next to your toilet for some light reading. Keep *War and Peace* on your shelf and *The Importance of Being Average* on your toilet.

I think your night stand might be too important for this book. That's where you *get serious* about reading. So rather than risk this little book having more influence than it should, I suggest you keep it out of the bedroom altogether. Let it live in those areas of your house reserved for *light* topics.

Now, what if this becomes an audio book? *Where* are you allowed to listen to it? Well, I think it's safe to say that you are not allowed to use any type of portable player for it—that would mean you are too into the book. I'm also going to say you can't use the home stereo for the same reason. That really leaves us with two choices of where you are allowed to play the audio version of *The Importance of Being Average*. You can play it in your car and you can play it on your computer. But—and this is an absolute must—you are forbidden from staying in the car to listen to it once you have reached your destination. This audio book *cannot* get your full attention. It must be listened to only when you are moderately distracted by other things such as driving or working on the computer. In that spirit, I suppose you may listen to it with headphones, as long as you are cleaning the house or organizing your CD collection.

The Importance of Being Average

There are a lot of *great* books in the world. And you might read them while you're eating a ham sandwich. If that was the case, I'd tell you to focus more on the extraordinary book than the ham sandwich. But do me a favor while you read *The Importance of Being Average*—focus on the sandwich more than the book. Use another book to define the greatest moments in your life—use this to get more out of a hot fudge sundae with your kid.

You need the right *level* of emotion reading this book. You can only see average when you aren't trying too hard to see it. Sometimes when you focus too intently you miss the point. Sometimes a whisper in your ear that you barely hear can change your universe...barely listen to this book.

And just because I'm whispering to you, that doesn't mean I don't care about the message...just the opposite, in fact.

Take this book *less seriously* than a book that will change your life...it just might be the book that does.

John Grace

Meeting Average

Hello. And welcome to yourself. I know you said a lifetime ago that you were going to grow up and be something special. But that didn't happen, did it?

So you're stuck, stuck in the rut of mendacity. You're average. Middle-of-the-road. Nothing special. C. C+ on a good day. You're not pretty. Not ugly. Not rich. Not poor. Here you are. And here is where you are going to end up. Nobody. Nobody spectacular.

If that seems depressing, then I'm glad you're here. I hope you can learn to be *proud* of yourself as a nobody. Believe it or not, I am proud of you. I know you're nothing special and I'm still proud of you. I've fallen in love with the unspecial people of the world—I'm going to try to convince you to do the same.

Being special is over-rated. Who needs that kind of pressure? Life is hard enough without the expectation you have to be *good* at it. Just think of how much easier your life would be if your *goal* was to struggle, if each day you tried to be average, to do nothing out of the ordinary.

What if you said to yourself each morning, "Today, I'm going try to be just like everyone else. The world is going to kick my ass and I'm going to learn to smile about it."

I could do that—I'm good at getting my ass kicked by the world.

I've lived a lifetime *trying* to be special. It's never worked. Oh sure, there have been a few moments here or there when I've achieved something exceptional. But there is always enough middle-of-the-road waiting just around the corner to remind me, "John, you really aren't that good at life."

I may be a doctor, and that's kind of special, but believe me there is more than enough mediocrity in the rest of my life to compensate. If I'm being a good father, I'm neglecting my business. If I'm taking care of my health, I'm letting the house go. If I'm keeping up with culture then I'm not keeping up with the lawn. Whenever I am doing something well, I'm doing something poorly. In essence, it all averages out to a pretty run-of-the-mill performance in life.

No matter how many times I hit the reset button and say, "Okay, from this day forward, I'm going to do it all well. I'm going to give a good performance across the board." It never works out that way. Even this book is a white flag for me. I already tried to write the Great American Novel, the book to change the world.

Nobody wanted to read it.

Since that didn't work out—I'm lowering the bar. I've found lowering the bar is an easier way to achieve my goals. Rather than trying to write an epic novel that changes the way mankind views himself, I've decided to write a below average manuscript that a few people will enjoy.

Problem solved. I can guarantee *this* book will be a success. You have to love the power of *decreasing* your expectations.

I considered a lot of titles before settling on *The Importance of Being Average.* Some other options were,

Lowering the Bar!
Striving to Be Normal.
Fail!
Mediocrity Rules!
Be Like Everyone Else.
Jump Lower!

The Importance of Being Average

A Mundane Kind of Special.
Everyday-ville
Don't Be an Over-achiever!

I like them all. I think you get the idea. Each of them pokes fun at our selfish individualism.   They all take shots at narcisstic, iconoclastic, 21st century America.

But *The Importance of Average* suggests something more. It suggests not only is there something destructive in trying to be special but there may also be something worthwhile in being average. Average may have a few tricks up the sleeve. There may be something important in normal. We aren't as special as we think we are, but maybe average is better than we thought it was. And this book may end up taking you somewhere special by taking you somewhere that you go every day.

***

My quest for the average began like any other day. I woke up, weighed myself, showered, shaved, and went to work. I came home, kissed my wife, ate dinner, played with my daughter and put her to bed.

And as I lay in bed with my daughter on my arm, staring up at the stars cast upon her ceiling from her nightlight, I thought, *John, when are you ever going to do anything amazing?*

I thought about it. Clearly, by the age of thirty-five, my hopes of being a professional athlete were over. I didn't really see myself breaking into Hollywood, or modeling, or the music business. I didn't think I was smart enough to make a lot of money. And even if I got lucky and made a lot of money, I didn't think I was smart enough to keep it. You have to be pretty clever to hold on to any amount of cash these days.

As I crossed more and more opportunities to be special off of the list, it slowly dawned on me that I wasn't really going to do *anything* spectacular with my life. I asked myself,

"You mean I'm not going to be spectacular?"
"You mean I'm not going to be famous?"
"You mean that everybody isn't going to know my name?"

Then I realized. *Yeah. That's right, John. That's exactly what I mean. You're going to be a minor cog, in a minor machine, in the middle of nowhere. Just like all of the other nobodies.*

I felt a twinge of sadness, a dash of regret, a teaspoon of sorrow with just a sprinkling of guilt on top. I didn't care for the feeling. But I couldn't think of any way to remove it. The only thing that came to mind was to actually go out and make something of myself. I'd already come to the conclusion that was just *too* hard.

But then it popped up. And I said it. It just came out. I didn't really think about it. *Well, I could just be happy with being average?*

I don't know *where* it came from. My first instinct was revulsion—to slap myself for such blasphemy. It was anti-American. Sacrilegious. Fool-hearty.

Not be special? Everyone always told me I was special. My parents let me win at games. Grandma and Grandpa said I was the "best kid in the world." How could I let them down? How could I let myself down? Nobody ever got C's in my school. C's were for the losers. Average was for losers. Average was bad.

***

The Importance of Being Average

Unfortunately, we have to take a break from our story. My average life is taking center stage now. And rather than put off my average life—I'm letting it into the book.

My daughter was running while playing her plastic flute last night and—you know the rest of this story—we're on our way to the doctor's today.

This isn't anything dramatic. It isn't anything unique. It's one of those day-to-day injuries that happen to millions of kids across the world every day. Here I am on my quest to do something special sidetracked once again into the muck and mire of everyday existence.

Of course, if I'm happy being average then I'm really *ecstatic* right about now. If it's my goal to be like everyone else—I'm a heck of a success. I'm hanging out in the car, talking to my wife, taking my kid to the doctor for an unexpected injury that occurred, rather than getting to my plans of worldwide success through writing this book.

Life happens while you are making plans. And my life is always less exciting than my plans. And the question is whether I am going to be happy or miserable when life happens. Am I going to care more about the life or the plans? The plans tend to be amazing—the life always ends up average.

Starting to see the theme here?

***

So my wife had me read the first few pages of this book to pass the time, as we drive to the doctor, to repair the kid, who fell on the flute while being irresponsible in the living room, thereby ruining my plans to achieve something spectacular with my life today.

Her response was, "It's cute. I'd read it. Could you scratch my back?"

John Grace

It's cute? It's cute! Did anyone ever tell Steinbeck or Hemmingway their writing was cute? Did the Vienna Society of Physicians look at Freud's work on the Ego and the Id and say, "Gee, Sigmund, that's a really *cute* way of looking at the mind?"

Did someone look at $E=mc^2$ and say, "Hey Einstein I think the speed of light is really cute in that equation?"

Cute. Cute? Cute is a very average word. There it is...average...*again.* Averageness is permeating every second of every day. Of course, if being *mundane* is a goal then I'm excelling.

"Jeff is tiling their bathroom today." My wife says later in the conversation. Wow! That's exciting.

No! No, it's not exciting at all. It's average. It's boring. It's. It's. It just is — that's all. I want to run away. Get out of the way. Get out of my way. I've got to get myself on a pedestal. I've got to go find a mountain to climb so that I'm taller than everyone else. I can't stand these trips into normalcy.

No. No. Bad John. Remember. We are going to try and have fun being average.

Woo hoo. Yee haw. Okay. I can do this. I can enjoy the average things. I can enjoy the nothing. I can have fun with all the stuff that doesn't really matter.

I suppose I'll just start by taking a deep breath. Look at my wife. Look at my daughter.

Here is my wife sitting next to me in the car. We've been together thirteen years. It hasn't all been good. It hasn't all been bad. Most of it has been pretty average.

But when I look at her, when I think about those moments. When I think about her having our child, holding my hand, or feeding our baby, it doesn't feel bad.

If I could get average to feel like this, I think it could be pretty darn satisfying.

Then I look at my average kid. She's in the back seat with a cut on her lip, sleeping with a bear in her arm, wearing a little pink hat and matching sunglasses—just like a million other kids riding in a million car seats on their way to a million doctors. Nothing special. Average—my average. That average doesn't feel too bad either.

***

It's been a while since our culture celebrated average. Tom Brokaw had a book a few years ago, *The Greatest Generation*, where he talked about the group of Americans that fought in World War II and rebuilt the country following The Great Depression.

Woops. My average life is here again. My daughter is now crying in the back seat because her mother just went into *Target*. Now if this isn't a snapshot of everyday life, I don't know what is.

I'm trying to soothe her, trying to calm her. "It's okay baby. Mommy will come back soon. It's okay. Daddy is here."

She keeps crying.

I'm inadequate, pathetic, wallowing in the age-old problem that fathers watching children have faced for the last millennium. *How in the heck do I keep this kid from having a meltdown?*

Finally, mom comes back and I feel like I just found a water fountain in the middle of the Sahara desert. *Saved! Thank God! Thank you God! Thank you for mothers! Life would be pretty impossible if I had to raise this kid by myself!*

There is nothing different about this, nothing special. I'm average again. 50th percentile. Right-in-the-middle, just like all the other dads out there who have no idea what to do the instant mom steps out of the room. Mission accomplished. Destination reached. Next stop: Everyday-ville. Just to put the icing on the cake, just to put the final nail in this very ordinary coffin, the next place we stop is *Starbucks,* which is quintessential Americana for March 23rd, 2007. There is nothing more normal these days than a trip to *Starbucks.* Everybody does it. Everybody else is here. Everybody is doing the same thing. And here I am being quite *amazingly* average. We may as well stop at *The Gap* on our way home.

Suddenly I hear from the back seat, "Hey. Hey you. Hey dad! Hey. HEY! Could you get my teddy bear?"

My daughter can be kind of pushy.

"You dropped your Teddy bear?" I reply. *Can't you see I'm working on something special here?* You see this book is the only slightly unique thing going on in my life. So I gravitate to it like a drug. But normalcy keeps creeping into my fantasy— ruining my high. And I keep being ripped back to here and now. *Here and Now* is a long way away from *Happily Ever After.* The normal story of my life keeps talking over the fairy tale.

"Hey. Hey you. Hey dad. Could you get my Teddy Bear? I NEED it! I need my Teddy Bear." She asks again.

I chew on my cheek for a second. Then, after a deep breath, I think. *Enjoy the normal story. Enjoy it. Enjoy the average. Enjoy being like everyone else. Immerse yourself in the day-to-day existence, in the madness that is 21st Century America.*

Then I smile and I say to my daughter in my best goofy voice, "Well, why do you need this Teddy Bear?"

"Because I do. Because I do. Because my mommy say so. That I need it. I need him and he fell down. He fell down there. And I have to go to the doctor and fix my mouth and I need my Teddy Bear. Will you get him?"

"Sure." I say. "I'll get your Teddy Bear." I start laughing then I reach in the back seat, grab the bear by the ears, and gently lift the small stuffed animal into Amberly's eager, outstretched hands.

"Hooray!" She screams.

I've saved people's lives and they haven't been that excited. Grabbing a Teddy Bear may be the most interesting thing that I do today. It may be the most interesting thing I do this week.

It may be the most important thing in my life. How much of my average life have I been running from? How much have I been missing?

***

I like to think of this book as slightly funny. I consider myself a funny guy. I would consider myself a riot but that wouldn't fit into our theme. That would be me trying to sneak special into my life again.

But there's that little voice that keeps whispering into my ear, "But you are special. You really are special John. Mom and Dad were right. The whole world is wrong. That's why you haven't been discovered. That's why you're not famous."

I like that voice! But it also makes me angry because then I want to say, "Well what the heck is wrong with the world? Can't they see I've got some mighty clever stuff going on here? Come on! When are they going to catch up?"

But then there's another voice that says, "Well maybe, just maybe. I hate to burst your bubble chief. I'm real sorry to break this one to you, John. But perhaps, just perhaps, the *reason* you haven't done anything spectacular is because you *aren't* that spectacular."

Ouch! That really smarts! This embracing average is going to be tougher than it looks.

I certainly gave one heck of an average performance at lunch today. I sat down, told myself I was on a diet, promised not to eat too much, then ordered a monster cheeseburger with onion rings. Feeling guilty, I left one onion ring on my plate but still managed to eat half my daughter's breakfast and all my wife's hash browns.

That's how most people do diets—a good average lunch performance.

I followed this up with a remarkably common display in *Walgreen's*. Strolling the isles looking for my daughter's medication, I asked an employee for directions. She was young and attractive so I sucked in my stomach, walked with a bit of a swagger, and convinced myself, *Yeah. She likes me.* I knew this because attractive young twenty-year-olds have a hard time meeting balding, overweight, middle-age men with wives and sick three-year-olds.

While this story doesn't exactly make me a knight in shining armor, I'm pretty sure I'm not the only guy on the planet that enjoys being a little delusional about how attractive they are to the opposite sex from time to time.

So there it is again—average. And boy I am good at it.

***

This time I really am going to talk about Brokaw's book because there is a mildly interesting point to make. I would say an important point if I considered anything I'm saying to be important. But I tried to write the important book and like I said—I've lowered the bar.

Brokaw talked about the greatest generation in American history and how much they did for the country and how much we owe to them. He talked about the heroes of Normandy. He talked about the giants of industry. He talked about the values that laid a foundation for rebuilding everything that we lost in the Great Depression. And he talked about these things with sadness and longing, like they were gone forever, an anomaly that we will never see again.

I've met a lot of people from that generation. I've seen them in my office. Like I said—I'm a psychiatrist.

And I think that means that we have to get sidetracked just one more time while we talk briefly about my job. And I promise the next time we come back to Brokaw's book I'm going to finish this mildly interesting point.

But on to my job, yes, I am a psychiatrist. I sit in a room and talk to people all day long. Not really *crazy* people. Most of my patients are fairly normal—I specialize in normal people struggling to deal with a crazy world. People always blame *themselves* for losing their mind—I blame the world.

"How did I get here doc? How did my head get in this place?" They might ask.

"You were born." I answer. "You were born with a reasonable desire to make sense of things and born into a world that doesn't make much sense."

So my patients and I spend a lot of time talking about how to think reasonably well in a world that doesn't have a high opinion of sanity.

And as I write this, I realize that most of the world isn't going to think much of my quest to enjoy average.

But it's not that I *want* to be average. It's not that I'm *excited* about the idea. I'm just trying to embrace the truth because whenever I hop onto the magic carpet ride of self-indulgence, I end up smacking into a brick wall. The world reminds me again and again that I am *not* amazing.

I stand in line like everyone else. I overeat. I get frustrated at my kid—like everyone else. And every day I wake up and I wish I could do a better job at life—just like everyone else who is living.

My performance always comes up short of my expectations. My dreams always outstretch my capabilities. I'm just trying to stop hitting those walls of frustration—trying to make my life a little easier.

But this whole side discussion was to mention my job and tell you that I talk to a lot of people. I think that makes me an expert on what is strange and what is normal.

I've gotten to know a lot of people from Tom Brokaw's Greatest Generation. I've sat down with them, picked their brain, seen them laugh and cry. I know what they regret, what makes them smile and scares them—I've seen who they *really* are.

You know what the funny thing is? Do you know the one word that comes to mind when I think of them, the one word that sums up the greatest generation in American history?

Average

Nothing special. Middle-of-the-road. Not too bad. Not too good. Just doing my job. Just getting by. That's how they saw themselves. They weren't ashamed of it. They weren't afraid of being average. They weren't ashamed of washing dishes.

That's what made them great. The janitor of the rivet factory took pride in his average job. The mother of three wasn't miserable when she didn't have meat for dinner. She was just like everybody else—sacrifice was a part of life.

There wasn't a panicked scramble to escape the mundane. Life was hard for everyone and that made it okay to be hard for you. People weren't *ashamed* of struggling because everybody struggled.

Somehow that got lost. And it got lost in my head too. And I got the crazy notion that I had to grow up and do *something* with my life.

I suppose the baby boomers spoiled us. They wanted to make sure that we didn't struggle as much as they did. But they never realized—their struggle made them great. It made them average.

As more and more time goes by I realize that special isn't going to happen for me. Or maybe it is happening and I just don't notice it? Maybe I'm doing more than I think? Maybe I am that janitor in the rivet company who helps save the world by picking up the trash on time? Maybe the most important thing I can do is keep focusing on my average life and stop running away from it? Maybe the trick to life isn't about separating myself from everyone but rather falling into line, regressing to the mean, slipping right into that 50th percentile and loving the fact that I am no different from the other five billion people on this planet?

***

Now I'm sitting in *McDonalds*, watching a mom feed her baby. The little blond girl looks like my little girl. She's wearing pink ribbons just like my daughter does.

Her dad comes to the table and plays with her. She smiles at her father and laughs. Then he smiles and laughs. Then I smile and laugh.

It's pretty boring. But it's the best part of my breakfast. But no one walks up to that little girl and says, "Hey! Aren't you cute? Maybe some day you'll be a postman? Or work at a gas station? Or struggle with your mortgage?"

I suppose those hopeful parents would be quite angry with me if I were to say those things. Although, I must admit, I am *tempted* to do it because they wouldn't be angry if I said, "My goodness! What a *beautiful* little girl! You're the prettiest girl I've ever seen!"

Parents are fine being told their kid is special but get upset if they're told their kid is ordinary.

Ordinary is an insult.

You see this sort of thing at parent-teacher conferences. Between these little pow-wows and peewee league sports we have the initial war against normal beginning. There is a silent battle against average that starts with kindergarten parent-teacher conferences and continues right up through the homecoming court. We don't like average—we learn that early and repeatedly.

I did well in kindergarten and was thankfully saved from the brand of shame that accompanies a "performing as expected" verdict at the parent-teacher conference. But I remember the boys and girls, lined against the wall holding their little report cards, and it was easy to see who was "performing as expected", who was "above average", and who was "exceptional."

Even early in life, average was a curse. I remember the vacant stares of the other five-year-olds as they waited in line for judgment against their mediocrity. As T.S. Elliott so eloquently described the masses more than half a century ago, they were *The Hollow Men,* doomed souls destined to plod through life as misfits of fate, shackled to a rock of ineptitude and sinking from the cream of the corn.

I was happy that I wasn't one of them.

But I've learned how wrong I was. Nobody told me we all end up average. Nobody mentioned that my potential was ordinary. Even today, I get a "C" in my life.

I get an "A" in biology. "B" for reading lab results. "D" for sticking to my diet. "C" in parenting. Put it all together and I'm nothing special. But why is that so bad?

The Importance of Being Average

Why does it make me so angry?

When did average become an insult? When did we decide, "What is good enough for everyone else isn't good enough for me?" How did we come to that conclusion?

Because the *day* that average wasn't good enough was the day most of us started not liking ourselves…and after that day we started not liking *most* of the people living on this planet.

***

On to my quest to embrace the mundane, to relish in commonality, to celebrate that really fat part of the bell curve.

I find I get a lot more aches and pains as I get older. I'm pretty sure that makes me right at home with the rest of you. I doubt there's anything too unique in dealing with the fact that your body breaks down.

Getting older means getting average. There isn't anything special about aging. Whatever small piece of special you have tucked away is going to be chipped away as time moves on. The *amazing* stuff is the stuff that gets hit hardest.

This is one of the tougher things to accept about this whole average thing. I don't really care for pain all that much. It may not be an allergy but it's a pretty strong aversion.

So as much as I'm starting to love average, I think I would be okay if I wasn't in an average amount of pain. If there is one area of life to be special in—that's it.

Forgive me for wanting to be different, but I don't want the pain that comes with aging. And the funny thing is, I think that makes me like everyone else. I don't think any of us deal with deterioration very well.

Does being scared make me average? How about laughing when I'm scared? How about helping other people to laugh?

Yeah—that is a good feeling. Making my daughter giggle is one of the best things I do. I think we all enjoy making other people smile. Too bad we don't do that more often. I hope to make a few people I know smile with this book. As a psychiatrist, I spend my day trying to help people smile. I spend my life in a little room. The room doesn't change much. I don't change much. But it isn't boring because sometimes the people coming into the little room change a great deal. My patients keep that little room interesting.

There isn't enough humor is there? Isn't enough laughing? For being stuck smack dab in the middle of craziness we sure seem to take ourselves too seriously, don't we? For not being able to control a damn thing, we sure try to control everything.

***

A lot of average people have rolled through my life. A lot of nobodies have walked down the catwalk of my personal fashion show. They have worn a lot of different hats and a lot of different outfits.

Father. Mother. Teacher. Friend. Girlfriend. Bully. Wife. Kid. They have all been there. Each of them has taken their turn on the stage of my life. And there's nothing special about any of them. They are minor players or non-existent extras in the story of the world and could be written out of most people's lives without anyone missing them.

But they are the cast in *my* play. In their average, ordinary way, they have created my world—defined my life—painted my sky and colored my trees. They make the air smell like flowers in the summer. They are the reason I step forward and the reason I step back. When I think of everything that means anything—I think of them.

The Importance of Being Average

They are nobody special. Average. And the world's "average" defines my world.

They don't *feel* average to me. In fact, if I ever became special, if I ever did do anything *amazing* with my life. The only part about that would mean anything would be whatever corner of special I could share with them.

My Courtney. My Amberly. My Uncle Paul. Aunt Nancy. Sandy and Mark. My Granny. My Mom. My Dad. Johnny and Debbie. Brian and Elizabeth. Rachel, Curt, Aaron, Vic and Brad. Dayna and Jeff. Jeanie and Laura. Karen. Donna. Viola. John. Robyn, Tish, Doris and Larry. Glen and Kallie. Julko. Bob. Christopher. Victoria. Jonda. Kevin. Matt. Melissa. Donna and Steve. Gloria and Sean. Patty, Roz, Debbie. Eric and Kathy. Gene and Kaye. Mike and Kimberly. Darnell. Anna. Shelly. Kevin. Steve. Cindy. Maria. Alex. Jen. Andy. Matt. Terry. Edna.

Just names. Names on a piece of paper. You walk by them. You'd never notice them. But they are all that I have. They may not know it but they have built my life with small tiny pieces of average. That means something to me.

This book is written for the people you'd never notice. I want to let them know that they were noticed by me. I suppose that means I've been noticed as well. This book is about noticing all of the things in your life that never stood out.

***

Now it's Sunday. Work has piled up again. Should I go get some work done? I know that I should. I'm so behind. Again. Par usual. Nothing special in being behind. I don't think that's going to break into any AP bulletins.

"MAN FROM SMALL FLORIDA TOWN FALLS SLIGHTLY BEHIND IN HIS WORK"

Boy, that's a real page-turner. Heck, while we're at it lets put up the headlines from the last three months of my life.

"DISGRUNTLED SPORT FAN UPSET THAT HIS TEAM DIDN'T MAKE THE PLAYOFFS."

"BUISINESS OWNER FEELS GOVERNMENT MAY TAKE TOO MUCH IN TAXES."

"NEW YEAR'S RESOLUTION TO, "WORK OUT EVERYDAY" A BUST FOR FITNESS-CHALLENGED, FORMER SELF-PROCLAIMED ATHLETE."

"HUSBAND SAYS SOMETHING STUPID, ENDS UP ON COUCH."

"FATHER WORRIED THAT DAUGHTER IS GROWING UP TOO FAST!"

"IDIOT ACCIDENTLY DUMPS COFFEE IN HIS COMPUTER!"

We could go on and on. It doesn't get any more intriguing— these *are* the highlights.

Back to work. Or maybe back to bed? I'd rather go to bed than go to work. Maybe I should go to brunch? Should I go eat too much? Should I go play with Amberly? Should I give in to my impulses? Should I be normal?

You know the best thing in that list is going and playing with my daughter. But then there would be guilt. I'd have guilt because I wasn't finishing my work. Guilt is a very average thing. A lot of people have a lot of guilt. I guess that's why I have a lot of business. I spend a lot of time trying to convince people not to feel guilty about being average.

Shakespeare called jealousy a monster. I think guilt is a bigger one. I'm guilty more often than I'm jealous. In fact, I'm always feeling guilty about something. Guilt is like fear with no end in sight. It's worse than fear. It's fear with a little pepper on top. And at times it's a mild green pepper and at times it's a burning habanera.

Anyway, I've got my share of guilt. And right now, my share is sitting on top of me, telling me that I should go and do some work.

Fighting guilt is harder than giving in to it. That's why a lot of us get beaten down. A lot of us fight ourselves a significant part of each day.

Deep breath. Embrace the average. Embrace the mean. Forget about being good at life because you never will be good at it.

I know. I know. I never will be good at life. And *yet*, I KEEP TRYING to be good at it.

I'm really good at sitting on the couch and complaining about sports. A lot of people do that well. Too bad we can't consider that special in life. Then I would really be exceptional.

***

Okay. Fast forward. I decided to embrace the average. I didn't do any work. I got my wife flowers, my daughter ice cream, and myself a *York Peppermint Patty* and went home.

My wife smiled, not expecting me home. My daughter was thrilled, "Daddy! You were at work."

Then I showed her the ice cream and she started dancing. She did three turns, shook her hips and said, "Yea! Yea!" Then she grabbed my hand and let me into her room, "I've got a *big* surprise for you daddy!" She made me close my eyes, spun me around three times, and said with a huge smile, "Here!"

She handed me a pair of red swimming goggles.

I said, "Thank you." with a half-hearted, confused tone in my voice.

As if sensing my lack of understanding Amberly answered, "See, now you're like *Spiderman*."

I looked at the red and black goggles, put them on, and went to the mirror. There was a bit of a resemblance to *Spiderman*. That meant a lot because Amberly knows how much I like *Spiderman*.

What about *Spiderman*? *Spiderman* isn't good for average because he's pretty special. This forces me into a dilemma of trying to embrace average while secretly worshiping someone spectacular.

What am I going to do? I can't let go of *Spiderman*. Do I wish for him to lose his powers? Do I hope that he becomes one of the guys?

Heaven forbid, Peter Parker would walk into my office and say,

"Hey look Dr. Grace, the stress of the *Green Goblin* is really getting to me. I'm starting to get panic attacks when I go web slinging. My boss is this unrelenting jerk who constantly pressures me to get more and more done. My girlfriend just doesn't understand the sacrifices I have to make for my career. My Aunt May is sick and may not be able to live much longer at home. And the superhero's union just stopped their dental coverage!"

"Wow." I would say, "It seems you have a lot on your plate. And the whole proportionate-strength-of-a-spider thing isn't helping much. Maybe you would like some *Xanax*?"

That would be a tough conversation for me to have. I don't think I could tear down my hero for the purpose of building up my nobodies. So I guess I'm stuck again in the middle of a *Spiderman* dilemma.

Not really. I figured the whole thing out just five minutes ago. It turns out that it is going to fit really nicely into the middle of average.

The truth is, I never *cared* about *Spiderman* until my dad played superheroes with me in the sandbox. I never knew what color costume his costume was until my mom bought me *Spiderman* underoos. *Spiderman* was never special to me until my mom smiled at me while I watched his cartoon. It turns out standing behind this spectacular super-hero were two pretty average parents.

Average keeps getting better and better. I never realized how hard it was to see. But the more I see…the more I like.

***

Ditching work kept me busy the rest of the day. I did laundry. Amberly jumped into the basket and threw all of my shirts into the air. My wife lauded me with affection the entire afternoon for being home.

It was a good day, an average day.

Later Amberly and I went downstairs to pump up her flattened basketball she said, "Daddy you're so strong, you're my hero. You made the basketball come to life. You're like a doctor Daddy."

I realized that skipping work was the best decision I could have made. I finished the morning by having my daughter call my mom and dad. It made them smile. It made them laugh. I made two of the best people I know happy. I made *Spiderman* smile. Suddenly this very average morning felt a lot better than anything amazing I could have done at work.

Mirror, Mirror, on the Wall, Who's the Plainest of them All?

Plain Jane. Average Joe. Homely. Common. These are not words we prefer to hear when describing our appearance. There aren't any contests for the most average looking person. Nobody is giving out blue ribbons for looking like everyone else. I don't think I've seen anyone on *Top Model* sparkle when they heard, "We've seen your look a thousand times before." There is very little celebration of the average when it comes to appearances today.

I don't think you need to look different in order to look good. I don't think you need to stand out in order to stand up.

We're all trying to keep up with the Jims, the Joneses, and the Jim Joneses of the world. We're all trying to pack on enough silicone to no longer resemble human beings. We each seek to develop our personal cult of personality. The only fun way to be a member of a cult is to be the cult leader. Being a follower in a cult isn't anything that anyone aspires to. That's why cults have to trick people into joining. They trick them by convincing them they're special.

Maybe we're all followers in this cult called society, duped into believing that we're all special? The truth is there isn't anything unique about any of us. Why do we work *so* hard to deny that?

If this book is a little funny, you'll chuckle. If it's really funny, you'll laugh. If it is downright hilarious, you'll tell other people to read it. If enough people start laughing about the overall lack of special people in the world, it will suddenly transform *me* into one of them. If that isn't enough to make your head spin in one of those strange ironies of life, I don't know what is.

If this quest for the mundane is *too* successful, then it will be the ultimate failure. I haven't quite found a way to rectify that except to hope that people I know enjoy the book. I hope my average circle of friends and family like it. Truth be told, they shape my life more than the rest of the world.

I don't hope to be a champion for average because being a champion of anything pretty much takes you away from average. But I think we need to consider some kind of figurehead or spokesman for this new movement toward middle-of-the-road.

I don't know where to look for this new spokesman or spokeswoman for the nobodies of the world. *Superman, Batman*, and *Spiderman* are way too unique to serve as models for our president—although I'd slip *Spidey* in there if I could.

Captain Crunch while being a fairly salt-of-the-earth working man, still manages to fire cereal from a cannon from time-to-time. That takes him out of the running. You can forget *Peter Pan* and the *Energizer Bunny*. Anybody who can fly or is robotic tends to stick out.

Size, either too big or too small, is also a bit of deal breaker. *Mothra, Godzilla,* and *Tinkerbelle* will have to stick their respective venues.

I was thinking about someone like *Joe Camel,* who lets face it, has a very average, ordinary name. But although he claims, to be "one of the guys", I think secretly he is out there being pretty special. He tends to drive nice cars. Seems to be a good pool player. Most people in the room look at him. He doesn't exactly blend in with the crowd.

He's just not going to work.

Kato Kallen may have been a good choice prior to the whole O.J. Simpson business. What could be more average then a bleach-blonde out of work actor sponging off of his wealthy friends?

I'm not trying to tarnish his amazing reputation with the book. The truth is I don't know much about Kato other than he seemed like an average guy trying to be special.

I don't know if this is enough to get me sued. I'm not sure if we're allowed to talk about anybody in this country anymore. Even though we supposedly have free speech. Maybe if I put some sort of disclaimer like I don't really know what I'm talking about, then I'll be okay. I'll have to ask the legal department and get back to you. But for now…Kato is out.

If identical twins were more common then one of them would be really perfect. I mean who could be a better spokesman for the average movement than someone who didn't even have unique DNA.

That cloned sheep would be good, if cloning weren't in vogue.

I got it.

How about one of those genetically engineered seedless watermelons? That watermelon is essentially a clone to a million other watermelons.

If that isn't my spokesman, I don't know who is.

Fruit is an average sort of food. It's not chocolate. It's not lobster. It's not spinach. It's not broccoli.

It's middle-of-the-road. It's average. Most people like it—a little bit. And genetically engineered fruit has been around long enough to no longer be a novelty.

Watermelon isn't even that great of a fruit. It doesn't have a great name like Passion Fruit. Granted it is somewhat large.

But it is also fairly messy. Doesn't tend to be that sweet. Isn't a top seller. Watermelon is rarely used in cooking. Has a few big fans but not too many.

And yet watermelon is not obscure. Some people like it. Most people know about it. It does have a special place at 4th of July picnics but isn't fifteen minutes of fame part of being like everyone?

Watermelon is not a freak of the fruit world. It's not the kumquat. It's not the kiwi. It certainly isn't the ugly fruit. It's not deformed. Other fruit doesn't shriek in terror when it comes into the room. I don't envision a watermelon screaming, "I am not an animal!" to an angry citrus mob. I see it blending in with the crowd, fitting into family pictures, like your overweight, aunt Lucy.

Watermelon is a very average fruit. A cloned watermelon is nothing special. It isn't male. It isn't female. It just is.

And that is why our new spokesman for the average movement in the world is a cloned watermelon. That makes me smile. Maybe it's time to go out and get your watermelon t-shirt.

Oh. But the watermelon can't talk. It can't smile. It can't laugh. It can't have a face. And it certainly can't have legs. Walking, talking, smiling fruit is a big no-no.

The Kool-Aid Man is an extraordinary fellow. He set the stage for spectacular in my childhood, busting through walls and saying, "OH YEAH!" in his deep baritone voice. Our cloned watermelon can't be anything that special. It has to just sit there.

And what about uniforms? Should the average movement have some kind of insignia or dress code? I don't think so. Dress codes aren't *really* as average as they appear. They don't make everyone look like everyone else. They make it *easier* to stand out because all you have to do is deviate from the dress code in the slightest bit and suddenly you're a freak or a rock star.

So I don't envision us all in little *Star Trek* outfits with watermelons in place of a shiny starship on our chests.

***

American Beauty was on the other day and I've decided that's a wonderful movie for all of the members of the average nation. It should be required viewing for those of you attending *Average University*.

It was a good look at average in a positive way, apart from the murder in the living room at the end. My friend Aaron and I decided they should have taken out the murder at the end.

But I still give it a C. May favorite grade.

For Pete's sake, the penultimate scene has a paper bag blowing in the wind and we're all saying, "Wow, would you look at that!"

That's a celebration of average.

***

PB & J is average. And it fits right into the perfect food for this book. If you want to get any peanut butter or jelly on these pages—go right ahead. The book won't mind. Neither will I. We would both feel right at home with some Strawberry Preserves on the cover as long as you don't let any lobster, caviar, or hollandaise sauce anywhere near these pages.

***

So we have a movie, a spokesman and a sandwich. What else does the average revolution need? How about a song?

41

I don't want it to be too inspiring or anyone's favorite song. Bob Dylan is way too deep. Hendrix is way too talented. Faith Hill is way too pretty.

We need an average looking, average sounding, lounge lizard, with a simple message we've all heard a million times before. That's our anthem.

How about cheesy lyrics to an old song standard like *Rudolph the Red-Nosed Reindeer.* That's pretty good. Pretty plain.

Plain Jane

We are all just so plain,
And we're gonna stay that way.
We'll never amount too much,
But average can be okay.

All of the televisions,
Used to laugh and call us names,
They never let average kids,
Join in all their special games.

Then one average, sunny day,
Someone came to say,
Plain Janes with your clothes not right,
Won't you like your self tonight?

Then all the dreamers loved us,
And common people had dignity.
Plain Jane with no esteem,
Welcome to being happy.

Now that's a feel good song. And another piece to our revolution falls into place. As we prepare to march out-of-sync, in jeans, with food on our shirts, when we have a little spare time, to maybe talk to someone in a way that might get something done.

Average folks unite, with watermelons in hand, lack of consistent uniforms, an ambiguous message, and our minor hurdles to stumble over between breakfast and lunch. We have a date with mediocrity.

So the average movement marches forward . . . slowly.

We can't go too fast or it would be sensational. These ideas can't sweep over the country; they have to kind of trickle into a few little towns and cubbyholes. They have to be interesting enough to mention but not profound enough to change anything.

I'm walking a fine line here between sensationalism and obscurity and trying to land smack dab in the middle of nowhere special.

But I'm not trying too hard. I've got other projects to get to. Some day—I keep telling myself—I'm going to have time and energy to get to all of these projects I've got on the backburner.

But the truth of it is, I'm never going to do any of it. Everything that I'm *going* to do is pretty much what I'm doing right now—and I'm not doing much.

But isn't that the point? Appreciating average means enjoying what you're doing right now even though it isn't much...I'm learning.

John Grace

Men aren't from Mars Women aren't from Venus They're both from Iowa

Sorry Iowa. You were the most average place I could think of. But my point is that men and women are from the same place and it isn't *anywhere* as exciting as outer space.

I'm trying to decide whether there is a difference in the sexes when it comes to the pursuit of the ordinary. Are women more desperate to be special? Are men more driven to be unique? Is there something in the Y chromosome that screams, "Notice me! I am here." Or is that desperate plea for individuality recorded throughout the entire human genome?

In the sample of my life, men and woman seem equally focused on the spotlight. Both are drawn to a camera or microphone like moths to a flame. Both stare at their faces, bodies, and possessions in an effort to find whatever they can to stand out.

But men and women seem to handle fame a little differently. Men tend to get more women. Women tend to get better men. Women trade up. Men just trade more.

We all put our pants on one leg at a time. Each of us closes our eyes for a few hours at night. We all forget everywhere we've been. And everyone loses everything that means anything. We each think that moving forward is always a step in the right direction. And we all stumble while we try to keep marching ahead.

And yet despite these and countless other things that tie and bind each of us to every one of us, we focus on being 6'2'' instead of 6'1''. We focus on running a hundredth of a second faster than the second fastest human on the planet.

Our problem isn't that we aren't unique.
Our problem is that we think we need to be.

That's why I went on this quest to *enjoy* being like everyone else and stop running away from it because as I stand in front of *my* mirror—if I'm honest with myself—I can't see a damn thing that makes me any better than anyone. I'm so plain it hurts. So average it stings. So normal it's painful.

And my only salvation, the only possibility for walking through the rest of my years without feeling the burden of being one of the nameless, faceless unknowns in the world, is to fall in love with that anonymity—enjoy the averageness of my life and embrace the nobodyness of my time.

And that is the purpose of our diabolical revolution my friends. For you and I to wrap ourselves around white picket fences, minivans, SUV's, and too much debt with a little bit of pride. To look in the mirror at all that extra fat the average American is carrying and take a little satisfaction in the fact that we have plenty of company in our vices. We may not be exceptional but at least we aren't alone.

***

The other day I was swimming with my daughter and she was having me push her around the pool.

I'm giving up a lot of dreams recently. This book made me realize the end of those dreams and maybe the beginning of a mid-life crisis.

The Importance of Being Average

But as I looked into her big eyes that she describes as brown with a little bit of green, I told myself, *If I have to give up my dreams to get out of the way of hers then I'm okay with that.*

Each generation has to give up on itself. Letting go of being special becomes more important when you have kids. The day you have children is the day your dreams of special need to end.

We have to stop believing in ourselves in order to help our children believe in themselves. We have to let go of our dreams in order to help them find theirs. This has gone on for over a million years. Giving up on yourself is as average a thing as you can do. And maybe we could learn to embrace that average and do it with a little more pride?

That could be our jingle:

"I'm a quitter. He's a quitter. Wouldn't you like to be a quitter too?"

Quitting was good enough for my mom and dad. I'll be darn if it isn't good enough for my wife and I. It's not something to be ashamed of. The least we can do is give up on ourselves with a little pride.

I think mom and dad would be proud of their son who learned how to quit in life with a smile on his face. If you think that quitting with pride is easier than fighting to be special than you haven't tried to do it.

Quitting is easy. Loving yourself while you do it?
That's hard.

John Grace

Smelly Castle

Yesterday I was called home from working on the book by my daughter saying, "Daddy, come home! I have something to show you! You need to come and see my castle!"

Needless to say, I was intrigued enough to stop working. The entire drive home, possibilities entered my mind. *Did my wife buy her a castle? Did they build something on the porch? Castle certainly sounds expensive. I thought we agreed to talk about big purchases.*

I'm driving home, getting a little nervous and worked-up. Beads of sweat are forming on my brow. My heart rate is trickling higher. There is apprehension in my world.

As I pull into the driveway, I'm expecting a pink blow-up Barbie Castle sprawled over the yard. The Parthenon. Camelot. The Great Wall of China. But nothing is there. The yard is empty.

I breathe a sigh of relief. I walk up the stairs and into the house. Look around. Still—no castle. My wife is watching T.V. on the couch. My daughter is on the porch. It's a pretty ordinary picture considering the drama on the phone.

"Okay everyone! Daddy's here! Let me see the castle!" I actually go over the top because the two of them aren't anywhere near as excited as they had been on the phone.

My daughter walks outside, points to a pile of dog crap on our deck and says, "Here daddy. You need to clean this up. I don't like this castle."

Well at this point I know I've arrived in life. All of my dreams. All of my hopes. All of my expectations for life—I've exceeded them. I will never again doubt my success. No subsequent accomplishments could live up to being named to emergency dog crap duty. No matter what happens, nobody can take this away from me. My daughter thought enough of me, to call, interrupt what I was doing, and order me home so that I could clean up after the dog.

If that isn't the definition of respect, I don't know what is. Most parents fantasize about being mentioned in Valedictorian speeches. Some dream of poems on *Mother's Day* or Wedding proclamations. And "Hi Mom. Hi Dad." into a television camera is the *Holy Grail* when it comes to parental recognition. Parents dream and they dream big when it comes to their kids saying, "Thank you."

But those dreams are over for me now. I don't need them any more. I've got my recognition. Nothing says, "I appreciate the job you've done for me dad." like pointing me to a waiting castle of excrement. Forget flowers on Mother's Day. Don't mention ties on Father's Day. If you want to tell your parents you love them, get them a pooper-scooper and a place to use it.

If you're not laughing now, there's something wrong with you. How can I take myself seriously with this life? How can I have the faintest notion of competence or achievement?

This has got to be a joke right?

Yes. Yes it is. It is a *big* joke. And the funniest part of the whole thing is that I keep trying *not* to laugh. I keep focusing on the exceptional, spectacular, dramatic portions of my life when most of it is a ridiculous slapstick comedy.

My life is like the movie *Airplane* and I keep critiquing it like *Julius Caesar.* I say to myself, "Okay. Everyone. Let's get serious on the set of John's life okay? C'mon. Everybody let's get to some serious work."

Then a whoopee cushion goes off in the background or I get called home to clean up castles of crap.

The Importance of Being Average

Our lives are comedies. They aren't very funny if you try watching them as dramas. If you think of your life as a comedy, I guarantee it will not disappoint you.

Your life is either a good comedy or a bad drama. How are you watching it?

***

Well I am back from another journey into common. My wife dragged me out with her to the mall and *Target*. Now we're returning from that tireless procession to consume, to buy, to get even more stuff that we don't need.

That makes us just like everyone else. That feels good. Or at least it is *supposed* to feel good because I'm embracing average.

One of the stops in the mall was *Waldenbooks* and I was impressed by how many books they had to make me special.

Get an Amazing Body!
Master the Grill!
Use Every Second of Your Life!
Be the Best Father!
Be the Best Mother!
Teach your kid to be a Genius!

They were all there. Fancy book jackets. Clever color schemes. A lot of frilly people with really amazing teeth.

I didn't see any average looking books. I didn't see any average looking people on the covers. A lot of them looked *really* smart. A lot of them looked very hygienic. There were a lot of good bodies—fancy credentials and letters after everybody's name. I started to feel like my own letters: M.D., didn't mean that much anymore.

But even if those little letters don't mean much any more, they represent the biggest sacrifice in my life—they cost me nearly everything. I traded a lot of my average for a little bit of the world's special.

I didn't know it at the time. I didn't know how much I was going to lose. I didn't appreciate how much I *had* to lose. Only now that I'm embracing average, now that I value average, do I see how much was lost.

Christmas. Birthdays. Graduations. Conversations with family and friends. All gone because I was too lost in medicine, too driven by determination, too busy searching for special.

And five months before I graduated medical school, my father's car was pushed into a head-on collision when someone went through a stop sign. He spent the next three months in ICU. He'd never move his arms or legs again.

I sat by his hospital bed every day. I had nightmares. My stomach didn't work right. I'd never been more lost or confused.

When we dream about the future we imagine *everything* perfect, all our ducks in a row, each piece in its place. But there comes a moment in all of our lives when dreaming about the future changes. When no matter what happens from that day forth is, it won't be perfect. It's the day we lose the ability to dream about perfection and I remember the day it happened to me.

When my father lost his arms and legs, I lost the dream of "having it all."

The day you lose a big piece of your average life is the day you care a little bit less about perfection. You may dream about exceptional things but you mourn average things. I would give up every exceptional thing I have for my father to play with his granddaughter for an hour. I would give up all of my special to get back that single piece of average I've lost.

I don't regret going to medical school. I regret not appreciating my average life before I went. I wish I realized at the time how good I had it— playing catch with dad in the back yard on a sunny day.

Thankfully, I'm learning to appreciate average now. So that when the day comes I can't hold my little girl any longer, I'll know I appreciated it while I had it. Enjoy *your* average. That's what you're going to miss the most.

***

My biggest crime has been running away from a good life trying to build a great one. I wish I spent less time worrying about my grades in college and more time keeping in touch with my cousin Brian. I wish I spent less time in the gym trying to impress the world and more time drinking coffee with my mom. I wish I spent less time on special and more time on enjoying average.

This journey into the average has shown me just how special some average people are to me? I've never met a better person than my Uncle Paul. He's a hero in every sense of the word. Uncle Mark is the smartest guy I know. My friend Aaron is the funniest person I've met—he'll appreciate me saying that. Brad has the biggest heart. Mike is the most interesting. Glenn is the most dynamic. Nobody has overcome more than Aunt Jeanie. Rachel is the most fun to work with. Beverly and Paul are the kindest to strangers. My mom has the most faith in me. There's nobody more humble than my father. Dayna is the wisest person I know—she had life figured out when she was in high school. There is nobody who I want to impress more than my wife and nobody who I unconditionally love more than my children.

And my patients, who are they?

They know what I think of them.   They are the most courageous people I've met. You wouldn't know it if you met them. You might see them at a department store, as a teacher, or doctor, or lawyer, or even *McDonalds*. But you have no idea what they have been through. A good portion of this book is certainly dedicated to them. Being witness to their struggles, victories, and failures is the greatest honor of my life.

If this book helps just a few people I know to feel a little better, then that's all it needs to do. I'm proud of this little book. I'm proud of this little doctor. I'm proud of the sacrifice I made when I decided to put two letters after my name.

I just wish I appreciated the magnitude of the sacrifice at the time.   When you find average, you find how valuable your average life really is.

***

There isn't enough credit given to spill-proof coffee lids. They really help the quality of my life on a daily basis. And I'm focusing on all the little things that make life better.

But speaking of coffee, I just got ripped off for coffee again at the local gas station. And I spent a lot of time figuring out how not to get taken for a ride while buying a cup of coffee— twenty years of school *really* paid off.

I was trying to decide whether to buy the value mug for $2.99 or the extra-value mug for $4.99 or just buy my coffee in a Styrofoam cup.

I did the math and figured out how much I would save if I bought the $2.99 cup and how much I would save if I bought the $4.99 cup. In the end, I figured the only good deal was the

$2.99 cup and after five minutes of advanced algebra to save $1.36 I went to the counter and proudly offered my cup and credit card.

"Thank you sir, that will be $5.35." The clerk said.

"But I thought it was $2.99?" I asked.

"Oh no. We sold all of the $2.99 mugs. That will be $5.35."

They got me again. The world is kicking my ass again! I really am good at getting my ass kicked. And life is a lot more fun now that I take some pride in it. Average you are mine!

Some people pursue achievement. I'm pursuing enjoying underachievement. Some people work to do something with their life. I'm working on enjoying nothing. *It's hard work, John. But you can do it.*

If you can enjoy nothing...paradise is yours.

I went up to get some cream for my coffee at the coffee station. I saw a lady bring back two full containers of creamer and return them to the *public* container.

What is she doing? She already had those creams at her table. She might be trying to poison everyone. Those creams could make someone sick.

I wondered if I should do anything about it. I wondered if I should save everyone from getting sick from the next mass murderer who is running rampant in Crystal River gas stations and poisoning people with coffee creamer.

But then I realized. *John, your death isn't going to be any more special than your life. You're not likely to be murdered. You're probably going to die from heart disease or pneumonia just like everyone else. Why be so dramatic?*

You need to trust people more than that.

So I took one of the creams she left for myself and left the other one. It was a pretty good cup of coffee. No one died that day.

Free Samples of Psychotherapy

I hope you're having as much fun reading this book as I am writing it. I'm at *Panera* Restaurant right now, waiting for Amberly to finish cheerleading class. I've gone up at least four times to take free samples of bread off of the little tray in the lobby. I'm thinking of making it five but people are starting to notice my little trips.

Free samples and snow days are two of the greatest inventions ever, two slices of average life that most of us don't notice. We should all have more snow days.

You wake up. You expect to go to work. You get a big pit in your stomach. Then your boss calls before you hop in the shower and shouts, "Snow day!" Suddenly, you have the whole day off. Work would be a lot better for all of us if we had a few snow days every year.

And free samples should be everywhere for every kind of product. There should be people standing outside *Barnes and Noble* handing out single paragraph excerpts from books. There should be a little lady with *Shout* outside the laundry mat that cleans a spot off of your shirt as you walk by. I'd be willing to stand outside the office and shout one-liners of good advice as people drive by.

Every field, every industry should give free samples. Of course, there would always be people like me, going back five times for the sample. If I were giving out free samples of psychotherapy that would mean that some of the repeat offenders would keep driving around the block.

Of course, I could just start the free sample psychotherapy movement. I could start walking up to people in restaurants and say, "Hi. Would you like to try a free sample of psychotherapy with your meal?"

Or better yet. I could sell psychotherapy like a used car salesman—stand out front of my office with a big sign shouting, "I can psychoanalyze that brain for $19.95 today! Two-for-one special! You can talk about your mother and your father for one low price!"

I could also go the infomercial route and sell electroshock units. I'd have to get a shiny shirt and tie for that one.

"So you see folks we have a beautiful shock-o-matic here for your purchase.

That's right!

No more expensive trips to the doctor's office for electro-shock therapy!

Now you too can enjoy the experience of 10,000 volts coursing through your cranium in the privacy of your own home!

Note the fine European styling!

Sleek. Silver lines.

This model also comes in black, orange, red, and psychedelic pink."

There would be a lot of testimonials from people we paid off.

"My life used to be pretty boring until I got the shock-o-matic!"

"Shock-o-matic saved my marriage!"

"My dog couldn't stand to live with me until I got shock-o-matic!"

"Who ever knew electricity could be so much fun!"

"You heard em' folks! So don't waste too much time. We only have a few of these beautiful units left. They are flying off the shelves.

So call 1-800-electrocute-me and sign up for your very own personal electroshock therapy unit. Yours for just 300 payments of $299.00."

My point is that we spend too much of our time trying to come up with the latest-greatest schemes and not enough time enjoying the free samples in our average lives.

John Grace

An Average Easter Idiot

We went to an Easter egg hunt the other day and that meant bunnies, eggs, and candy. It also meant that some kid had to find the "Golden Egg" to get the extra special Easter basket.

As we hunted through the field with the multitude of other parents, I fantasized about *my* daughter hoisting the shiny egg above the masses like some beautiful heroine from Greek mythology. I kept the vision alive as long as I could until someone mentioned the precious treasure had been found.

After the hunt, I saw my little girl smiling with her basket full of eggs. She held up yellow, maize, and even orange eggs and said,

"There's a golden egg."

"There's another one."

"And another."

"See daddy. I got lots of golden eggs!"

I was struck with strangest conglomeration of average and exceptional within a person. My little girl thinks she's a princess. She believes she's charmed. She knows she can do magic. And in that field of grass with a thousand people she was convinced the Easter Bunny came just for her.

Just like every other parent, I let her keep believing that she's special, knowing that one day she'll need to forget it in order to be happy with herself.

Surprisingly, the more I like average, the more I like me. And the more I like me, the more I like other people. If you try to associate with the *best* of society that means you try to *avoid* most of society. And if you expect the *best* from your children, *most* of the time they'll disappoint you.

You need to learn to love *failure* in order to love your children because your children will fail at making life easy—all of us do.

***

If average humor is right up your alley then another Easter story will probably tickle your funny bone.

My daughter has a preference for girls because she identifies with her mother. As she states it, "Mommy is a girl. I'm a girl. Daddy is a boy. I like girls."

To which I question her from time to time, "Well what about Santa, Amberly?"

This always draws a dramatic and direct response, "Santa? Santa? Santa. Um. Santa is a girl daddy."

We go back and forth about girls and boys. I poke fun at her saying, "I like girls." Or, "I like boys." to get a response out of her.

If you're wondering whether this got taken out of context at exactly the *wrong* place, you're pretty clever.

We were at the Easter egg hunt. It was cold. We were getting bored. Amberly was getting feisty.

I started playing with Amberly and before I knew it I was shouting, "I like boys! I like boys! I LIKE BOYS!"

I'm not a particularly stupid man but I do tend to get a little wrapped up in playing with my daughter. My ranting must have continued for a good thirty seconds before my wife firmly grabbed my arm and said, "Hey! Would you listen to yourself?"

At that point my predicament dawned on me. I looked around at the dozens of parents surrounding me, staring with a mix of contempt, disgust, and confusion. What do you do in that situation? What can you do? Explaining really wouldn't have helped by that point.

I smiled. Swallowed my medicine. Picked up my daughter and whispered into her ear, "I like girls too!" Thankfully, the Easter egg hunt started before anyone had a chance to get really worked up. Parents might be interested in protecting their children from inappropriate comments but they are more interested in free plastic eggs and candy.

Easter egg hunts used to be more *fun* when I was a kid. There used to be more *hunting* involved. People would actually *hide* the eggs. None of this business where you walk into an empty field and just...pick them up. They shouldn't even call these things Easter Egg Hunts—they should call them Easter Egg Gatherings.

Imagine if deer hunting was like Easter Egg Hunting? You'd walk into a field of deer carcasses, throw as many as you can into the back of your truck, and then drive away.

Today's Easter egg hunts are disasters waiting to happen. Massive fields of eggs stretch out like fertile soil before the reaper's sickle. Greedy parents, dreaming of glory for their children, perch on the perimeter of a thin ribbon barrier waiting to pounce without a moment's hesitation at the first sign of a whistle, starting gun, or the word, "Hunt!" This is serious business for some folks and I've seen these hunts bring out the devil in mankind. Never have so many, sacrificed so much, for so little. Parents will forsake their dignity, their decency, and their children's safety for the opportunity to acquire one cent more of free, worthless, plastic garbage.

There is no choice but to view the situation as utter madness. Accept the madness. Embrace the madness—a little. Don't try to stop it, but don't become too big of a part of it.

And there you are. In the middle. Between extremes. We're back to average.

Average is about enjoying an Easter egg hunt without being consumed by it—even when you're making a fool of yourself.

***

I saw *Bill O'Riley* and *Geraldo Rivera* arguing on television last night. I was having a better evening than either one of them. When I compare my life to the rich and famous I think I have it better. Average Joe has it better. Famous people get more divorces, more diseases, more dysfunctional families, more drugs, and more contact with lawyers. That isn't exactly my top-ten list for Christmas.

What is it that we envy in this group? I'll tell you what it is. It isn't the money. It isn't the life. And it isn't the glitz in the hair or the white in the teeth. It isn't the phony parties, foie gras, or foreign film festivals. People don't care about all of those things.

But they do care about *recognition*. Famous people have recognition. They are acknowledged. They are important. People tell them that they matter and that matters to us. Being important means more than why you are important. Being noticed means more than reason you are noticed. There is no such thing as bad publicity so to speak.

But what if we *noticed* average? What if we paid more attention to our milkman than our movie stars? What if we started to like plain Jane instead of Cindy Crawford?

Ah…. the revolution of the boring begins.

Today is the day of the nobody. The dawn of a new era of mediocrity. Arise couch potatoes and overthrow the busy bodied, brown-nosed, over-achieving, over-arching oppressors ascribing to the cult of the superlative.

The Importance of Being Average

Fear not dear friends. For I know that you are lazy. I don't expect much from you in this fight. In fact, rather than actually ask you to care about anything, my only request to join our revolution is that you care less about something—care less about special.

Believe in your television remotes dear friends and your partially manicured, overly mortgaged front-lawn. Have faith in your potbelly. Trust in your academically challenged, over-hormone stimulated teenager. Believe in your ability to be taken advantage of by rich corporate sponsors and tricked by big insurance companies. Take a little pride in the fact you can read a contract a thousand times and still not appreciate how you are going to be screwed over once you sign it.

Don't worry. I don't expect you to do *anything* about *any* of this. I expect you to just sort of think about it, smile, and get back to watching television with a ham sandwich. Maybe you won't pick up the phone to buy the answer to all of your dreams from some infomercial.

Toll booths, fabric softener, talk shows, gas stations, hair coloring, paint, belt buckles, escalators, and picket lines. One small cross section of all of the unusual things we have to deal with, negotiate, and understand. And each of these add a little more burden, a little more weight to our average lives. But the average person trudges along, doing an exceptional job of handling each hurdle.

I take my hat off to all of them. And I take my hat off to myself because I have managed to ride a lot of escalators in my day and have never lost a limb.

Average is good. Average is great. Average is the power of this world. Exceptional does nothing without us. Nobodies make up most of this civilization. Progress is the product of the poor, penniless people of this planet plodding along. Our lives are defined by the nobodies not the somebodies.

Another wonderful thing about our quest to overthrow the narcisstic, psyche stretched across our landscape is that we don't need any leaders. We don't need any figureheads. (Although we can keep the watermelon.) We just need a lot of people that don't care about trying to be amazing. We need a mass of apathy. We need some people who take more pride in keeping their nose clean than getting their nose straightened.

And like I said, I'm not asking you to learn to be an average human being. I think you already know how to do that. I'm asking you to *like* doing it. Kiss your husband or wife and love the fact that they are a lot more average looking than Brad Pitt or Angelina Jolie.

Just when I'm taking myself too seriously, some keystone cop performance shows up and reminds me how lucky I am that I don't decapitate myself while shaving every morning.

***

I'm sitting outside in the *McDonald's* playground with Amberly right now. She just pointed up to the American flag and said, "Daddy, what's that?"

"It's the American Flag." I answer.

"Well what's it doing up there?"

"It's waving."

"It's waving to me? It likes me?"

"Yes, Amberly. It's waving to you. It likes you."

How lovely an image it is to have the American flag actually like us, each flag looking down on each member of this nation like some sort of benevolent spirit of our forefathers.

The desire for safety is an average thing. We all want to go to bed at night feeling that we are protected. The desire for security, for certainty is something we all share but none of us achieve. Complete safety is an illusion.

The Importance of Being Average

Another great moment just came my way I want to share with you. Amberly just ran up to me and said, "I want Paw-Paw to come with me on the slide."

"Paw-Paw" is Amberly's word for her grandfather, my dad, who was paralyzed and stuck in a hospital bed the rest of his life. He will never pick up his granddaughter. But Amberly doesn't think about that. She thinks of paw-paw as being a little cell phone that she can carry around. She calls him and walks around the house with him. She talks to him like one of her stuffed animals.

So rather than watch my daughter play with her grandfather, I watch her carry around a cell phone. She just carried it into a Jungle Gym and even slid the cell phone down the slide so that "Paw-Paw" could go with her.

That is a million miles from perfect but it's one of the best pictures I've seen in awhile. It's a neat story of some decent people working hard to make the best of a difficult situation. It's me enjoying average.

Well, *McDonalds* just closed the playground down on us and made my warm and fuzzy moment all cold and clammy. Average always comes in to bust up my *Kodak* moments. It's never quite like it's *supposed* to be. Life has a lot of moments of half-perfection. And halfway to perfection is . . . I'm not even going to say it—you know the word. But if you can add up enough half-perfect moments and you may just start to feel that life is pretty good.

This book is trying to show you how to add up all the *half-perfect* things in your life—you just might end up with more than you thought you had.

***

John Grace

Sitting here, I'm convinced that I had some really deep thoughts in the last twenty-four hours that I just can't seem to remember. I always think the thoughts I can't remember are the most important. But the truth is—I haven't thought anything *amazing* in the last thirty-five years. What are the odds that I forgot something really spectacular in the last twenty-four hours? Not very good.

Oh. I remember one of my deep thoughts and it wasn't one of my proudest moments. I was speaking to some friends the other day and they asked me how business was. I told them things were going well. They smiled and said, "Yep. There will always be *crazy* people."

I smiled and laughed a little and said, "You bet." But I felt a kick in my stomach. I couldn't stop thinking about the exchange the rest of the day.

Crazy People? Crazy People? Is that really what I think of my patients? Absolutely not. So why did I let that go? Why didn't I stand up for my patients?

I felt ashamed of going along with something I didn't believe because I've already told you that I consider my patients some of the most heroic people I've met. I made a silent promise to never let that happen again.

I guess regret is part of average. I was trying to be cool, trying to be special. That's why I didn't say anything. But the closer I get to average, the less I need to impress people. And the closer to myself I stay.

It reminded me of another time that special gave me a kick in the gut. I was at a grocery store with my dad who was being silly, acting out, and talking loud. I think he was trying to impress me, trying to show me he was still young, still cool.

A few people gave us looks. A teenager started to make fun of him. The teenager and I looked at each other and he kept making fun of my father. I laughed at his joke. I smiled while he made fun of Dad. He kept going and I kept laughing. We shared thirty seconds of humor at the expense of someone who had given everything he had to give me a better life.

Even though I was laughing, the truth was that I was scared. I was scared of some teenage kid and what he would think of me because my father was being loud in a grocery store. I was ashamed of dad. I was ashamed of me. And I was doing everything I could to impress somebody that I'd never met, even if it meant hurting someone I loved more than anyone on the planet.

Nobody is perfect. Nowhere is that more obvious than with people closest to you. You know all of their imperfections, all their mistakes. You can pick them apart any time for any number of reasons.

That's why loving average means so much, because it allows you to accept the faults in yourself and those closest to you and suddenly you're not afraid of teenagers in grocery stores anymore. You don't worry about the world seeing the little mistakes—you've embraced them.

It didn't take me long to realize what I'd done. I left the grocery store ashamed of myself and made a promise to never be ashamed of someone who loved me again. Of five billion people on this planet, very few of them care about me. I owe the ones that do respect and dignity, even if they turn out to be average people with blind spots.

I'm not going to be ashamed of average anymore. And I'm not going to let people call my patients crazy or psychos because the truth is, they're just average people. I'm really proud of the people I work with. I'm really proud of the work we do.

***

Amberly was quite annoyed with the Easter Bunny this year. On Easter morning, she kept finding eggs and shouting, "Hey. There's an egg. Hey! There's another one." And the tone of her voice gave you the idea she was ticked off at the Easter Bunny and seemed offended by his audacity to sneak into her house and leave eggs all over the place.

"Who the heck are you Mr. Bunny to just come in my house and throw your eggs around?"

Amberly and Court really enjoyed Easter. Amberly talked to my dad and mom. A big topic in their conversation was poking fun at me. It eventually got to the following chant,

"Throw daddy in the garbage!"
"Throw daddy in the water!"
"Throw daddy in the garbage!"
"Throw daddy in the water!"

They were all laughing about it.

And I'm thinking. *This is what I went to college, medical school, and residency for? For my three-year old, my wife, and my dad to say that I should be thrown into the garbage and into the water. That's almost as much respect as I got with the dog crap.*

But I enjoyed being ganged up on by three of the most important people in my life—even though they were poking fun at me and putting me in my place. They didn't call me doctor. They didn't call me sir. They called me, "Garbage boy."

But they said it the right way and every time they said, "Daddy, we're going to throw you in the garbage." All I could hear is, "We love you."

I took Amberly swimming later that day. We both pretended we were special. We imagined that we were superheroes and

70

had to save the land of the mermaids. We fought sharks, battled villains, and tackled giant sea monsters.

I just watched *Batman Begins* and *Casino Royale* so my imagination was in 5th gear and I was ready to save the world, even if it was in my own mind. And as I beat down the king of the sharks, and hoisted the crown of all mermaids triumphantly into the air, I couldn't help but be struck by the fact that I was *never* going to do *anything* this neat in life. My fantasy was always going to be more exciting than my reality. And I had the choice of either trying to turn my reality into some piece of fantasy, which seemed daunting and exhausting, or simply embracing the dream while I was dreaming and embracing the reality while I was living.

Dream big and live average. That's a good way of looking at life.

We unlocked *Dora the Explorer*, and we saved *Boots,* and *Mommy,* and *Barbie* from every sea menace imaginable, we hung out in the pool and looked up at the sky. I pointed out a plane flying to Amberly.

"What's it doin' up there?" Amberly asked.

"It's just flying. It's flying by to say 'Hi' to us. Say hi." I told her.

"Hi plane. Daddy, how we gonna get up there?"

"I don't know that's pretty high."

"Can we use a rope?"

"That's really high baby. I don't think a rope will reach."

"Oh. Okay. Well then I'll get my pink rope. It's really long. And I can jump really high too!"

I looked up at the sky and into my daughter's eyes. The trees were blowing softly in the wind. It was one of those quiet, peaceful days.

I realized that my daughter wasn't going to be alive forever and she was going to be a little girl for an even shorter amount of time. But rather than be terrified of the fact that things weren't always going to stay the same, I smiled because at least I was appreciating how they were in that moment.

For an instant in the history of all things, some carbon, some molecules, some water, and something special came together to make my little girl and let her play with me for a few hours on a sunny day.

I was shining a flashlight for one second, on one little piece, in one little corner in the averageness of the universe. Even this small piece of everything average was the most beautiful thing I'd ever seen.

PART II

SAVING AVERAGE

Life changed for me after that day in the pool. I didn't need to find average anymore. I could see it clearly.

I didn't need to try and appreciate it. I was in love with it. And I wanted to save it. I wanted to rescue average. I started to look at my life, the world, and my daughter's future with a new perspective, a new mission. Everywhere I looked, I saw people trying to do too much or go too far. I saw excess and extravagance.

Average was getting kicked to the curb.

There's a tinge of bitterness in the second part of this book, a bit of sadness that comes from watching average struggle in the world. There's a bit of preaching because I felt responsible to save average.

Please forgive that negativity. Don't allow it to disparage your opinion of average. Realize that deep down inside, I just wanted to save as much average as I could for that little girl in the swimming pool.

I didn't mean to take up the cause. It found me.

Enjoy part two of *The Importance of Being Average…Saving Average.*

Don't forget to laugh.

Laughing is the best way to save average.

John Grace

Our Average Society Tries Too Hard to Be Special

I heard they are thinking of making spanking against the law and I can't help but be proud of how far we've come. Nothing says progress in a society like the need for *more* legislation. We'll know we've reached the pinnacle of our civilization when we pass the first Toilet Paper Act is passed making it illegal to leave an empty roll of toilet paper in a bathroom. We should all start calling our congressmen demanding the first draft of the Act.

While we're at it, let's just cut to the chase. Let's regulate all offensive or destructive behavior. We should make getting eight hours of sleep mandatory. Eating too much for breakfast a felony. Watching excessive television a misdemeanor. Average parenting a fine. We should all be told how to live better lives so that we reach the promise of a brighter tomorrow. Regulation has worked so well in the past, why wouldn't we want more of it?

Laws raise children better than people do. Ideals are more important than average folks. Perfection means more than average even if perfection is a dream and average is a reality. Welcome to the world you dream of—the only problem is—you can't live here. The dreams of our society are better than the reality of its members. There isn't going to be anybody left after we remove all of the people that don't meet our outlandish expectations.

I like society. But I think it tries to be too special. I think it tries to do *too* much.

Our current technique for deciding what we should regulate is based on how nice it would be if we regulated it well.

"Wouldn't it be great if society could make sure no child is left behind?"

"Wouldn't it be great if society could stop violence?"

I don't see this as a rationale approach. It's like if you have a mentally challenged uncle who is a wonderful carpenter. And you say to yourself,

"Boy wouldn't it be great if Uncle Jim could teach me advanced Calculus and paint our deck?"

You're not really playing to Jim's strengths with those expectations. That's what we do. We constantly regulate and legislate based on excessive expectations of our abilities.

This conspiracy against average gets more insidious. If we were an average society we would have a lot lower expectations. We would have a lot less plans. We would have a lot less rules. But I'm not sure we would get a lot less done because we wouldn't bother doing things we don't do well.

To make this point, just imagine if we went in the entirely opposite direction. What if we tried to regulate more things we have no control over?

Let's start legislating lightning bolts? Lightning bolts kill a lot of people every year. Let's start a campaign to end death by lightning.

"SAY NO TO BOLTS!"

The Importance of Being Average

"No human being should have to go through the experience of half a million volts of electricity!"

"What is wrong with our world when we can't stop lightning bolts from coming out of the sky and killing our children!"

Let's make a department of excessive electrical discharge. Ban scooting across carpets in rubber shoes. Develop massive campaigns to keep people indoors during storms. Let's spend a lot of money on a lot of programs and bother a lot of people.

But guess what?

People will still die from lightning.

I see a lot of this. I see a lot of campaigns to end lightning in our society. We're far too special to be at the mercy of chance. We consider ourselves too good to be limited by our limitations. But maybe if we liked average, we'd be okay at not stopping lightning bolts. More of our resources could go toward doing things that we're actually capable of doing.

***

I'm discovering the government, the lawyers, and the propaganda machines aren't any better at creating utopia than the small average neighborhoods that we used to grow up in. And in the end maybe those neighborhoods were a better place to grow up because they didn't carry the expectation or promise of utopia. They didn't even try to be special.

If it sounds like I'm dark, if this ever sounds like I'm jaded, if you get the idea I'm bitter over the state of the world, you're getting the wrong idea. This isn't about condemning the world. It's about encouraging us to focus on what we can control and doing something reasonable about it. For most of you, it means less about dictating the way world politics should be run and more about raising halfway decent human beings and attending PTA meetings. It means connecting to the people you live next to more than some genius hosting a chat line five thousand miles away, taking a little pride while cleaning your garage, and giving a little respect while driving through *McDonalds*. It means noticing the janitor, and taking an average girl to the movies. It means not caring about cars, clothes, and houses more than the people who drive, wear, and live in them.

Looking at genocide on the History Channel, hungry kids on the Education Channel, and evaporating polar ice caps on the Weather Channel can leave you feeling pretty hopeless about the state of tomorrow. If you had to change all of that it would be so overwhelming that you wouldn't even *think* about it—and most of you don't because when you need to be special you tend not to think about things that overwhelm you. You ignore things that remind you just how little and average you are.

But maybe if we were a little happier with average, we'd be happy just doing a little. Then we'd all do a little and end up getting a lot more done.

Don't take this the wrong way. I have faith in us. The truth about us is more good than bad. I'm inspired by what we *do* manage to accomplish, particularly considering we accomplish it. Our achievements are impressive when you realize that human beings are behind them.

We're like a group of beavers building a dam. A beaver dam is not impressive compared to the Hoover dam. But when you learn it's built by beavers—it's inspiring.

That's how I look at society, at our world. If a perfect race flew by in spaceships and looked at Earth they would say, "My Goodness, that society is disgusting. How could anything that pathetic get built?"

And then one of the creatures might pipe up in the background, "Oh. No. You don't realize. Human beings built that society."

"Really?"

"Yes."

"Oh. Well for human beings that's not too bad. In fact, that's pretty impressive. They're kind of pathetic you know."

Loving average means loving the fact that we *are* pathetic compared to perfection. It means judging us within the context of our limited abilities as opposed to our unlimited expectations.

It means working together to build a good beaver dam instead of the Hoover dam.

We're just a bunch of dumb beavers.

***

Ergonomics is the study of work literally. But it is really the study of making life more efficient and suited to human beings. These are the people who make your keyboard raised so that you don't get carpal tunnel syndrome and your monitor tilted so that you don't get a crick in your neck.

My function as a psychiatrist is somewhat ergonomomical. I help people's minds deal with this crazy world. But I don't feel the world helps me. We don't have a psychologically ergonomical society.

Why do we have a forty-hour workweek for *everyone*? Why don't we have more jobs where you can work thirty, twenty, or even ten hours depending on your capabilities? Why don't we have more *natural* light in our environments? Why don't most jobs incorporate physical and mental labor simultaneously? Why don't we get to bring artistic endeavors to work? Why do we live life more like androids than humans?

I'll tell you why. We don't like average. We don't like ourselves. Look around and ask yourself this question,

"Was this world built with me in mind, or someone better than me?"

So struggling with this isn't easy and a lot of us have a hard time. Kids with ADHD are another example of average human minds struggling in a bizarre, artificial environment.

We give kids drugs so they can sit in school. Where did we get the idea that kids are *supposed* to sit in school? How did eight straight hours of concentration become normal?

What if we changed the rules? What if we suddenly required everyone to go two days a week without any sleep? What if that suddenly became an expectation?

Most of us could do it. Most of us could struggle and suffer through two days of insomnia each week. But there would be a few of us that couldn't handle that degree of sleep deprivation, a few of us would need to sleep for a few hours.

What would we do next? We'd label them with a disorder. We'd call it *Insomnia Preventicalis* and it would be a disorder of an inability to tolerate insomnia. We'd medicate those people with *Insomnia Preventicalis* so that they could function better under our new crazy requirements. That's how I look at a lot of our disorders.

If we loved average, we'd see our limitations clearer. We wouldn't be ashamed of them—and our limitations would be *less* of a liability.

I feel a lot of regret as I write a lot of prescriptions. But the thing that I regret most about writing them is that it's the right thing to do in this world sometimes. I'm often helping normal minds deal with our abnormal rules. The world is often sicker than my patients. But the world won't take medicine.

The Importance of Being Average

But if we loved average, we'd stop calling ourselves sick.
And we'd start changing the world.

***

Destiny is a great word. Literally, it means where you are supposed to go in life. But don't we all *really* imagine our destiny is somewhere special.

No one thinks of their destiny as working for minimum wage. You never see,

"Now hiring at Smart Oil. Fulfill your destiny to change oil for the rest of your life!"

No one thinks they have an average destiny but most of us, by definition, have average destinies. Your destiny is most likely to be nothing special. So embracing average is really fulfilling your destiny.

I lied down earlier this afternoon on a pillow we bought at *K-Mart* for $5.99. It felt pretty soft. The fabric was gentle and clean. And I realized that my cheap, average pillow was probably better than the finest silk bedding that Genghis Kahn had a thousand years ago. You might not be impressed with my $5.99 pillow but the Mongol empire certainly would have been.

Average is pretty good if you look at it in the right way. And I drifted off to sleep—happy I was fulfilling my average destiny to sleep on a cheap pillow better than Genghis Kahn's.

One day I'll rummage through the rest of my treasures: clean sheets, fresh clothes, and a soft bed. I'll find what else I can rub in the faces of all the famous conquerors in the past.

If I can see how special I have it compared to the hundred billion people that have lived before me, maybe I can accept how average I have it compared to 260 million other Americans living with me.

We all have it special compared to everyone who lived before us. For most of us, that isn't enough. Look at our appearance. Everyone in modern America is more attractive than everyone living a hundred and fifty years ago. Our teeth are whiter. Our clothes are cleaner. We're taller, healthier, and wealthier. If any one of us went back in time, we'd all be worshiped for our beauty.

But instead of appreciating all of the progress we have made, we look for any excuse to tell ourselves we're not good enough. We're a society full of Adonises and we can't stand to look ourselves in the mirror.

It isn't our appearance that repels us. It's our disdain for average. Remember that the next time you look in the mirror. You just might be pleasantly surprised.

I slept that afternoon dreaming of winning every beauty contest a thousand years ago and I realized that every girl I saw today was more beautiful than the face that launched a thousand ships.

My Life is a Joke
I'm the Punch Line

I was at *McDonalds* with my shirt un-tucked, my hair messy, and a ketchup stain on my pants. There were several high school students sitting in a corner. They were having a good time, laughing out loud to one another. After a few minutes, I realized they were laughing at me.

I started to get a little ticked off, upset. Part of me wanted to confront them. *This is what I work my butt off for? So I can come here and be treated like this? Who are these kids? Who are these punks? Why doesn't anybody have any respect for anyone any more?*

Then I realized. *You know, they're right. I am a joke. And they don't even know the half of it. Sloppy hair? Food-stained shirt? If they really wanted to see some incompetence they would look at the rest of my life.*

I should have walked up to them and said, "Hey guys, I know my sloppy appearance is funny, but this is just the tip of the iceberg. If you think I'm incompetent at getting dressed, you should see me try to balance my checkbook. Or better yet, come by my house and watch me try to discipline a three-year-old. Then you'll have great material."

When you love the average side of yourself, the insults roll off your back a little easier. It's easy to insult average people but hard to bother them if they love being average.

I enjoyed my double cheeseburger while the high school kids enjoyed my ketchup stain.

John Grace

***

There's a banner at Amberly's gymnastic class that says, "Laziness is getting tired before you do any work." Every time I see that banner I feel lazy. And I wonder why I feel so lazy when I seem to be working so much.

I remember in high school thinking that going to work every day seemed awfully hard. Working most of the day, every day, for a lifetime seemed like a real accomplishment. And I'm realizing that even an average performance takes a *lot* of effort. Life isn't easy. Or at least it doesn't seem easy. Why not? Why doesn't life seem easy?

Life is smooth in a lot of ways. *McDonalds* makes a smooth cup of coffee. Eating breakfast is simple. Finding clean water is a piece of cake. When I say these things, they seem like important things. Yet, I don't appreciate them.

I don't wake up every morning and say, "Thank goodness I didn't have to hunt a pig for bacon this morning." I never think to myself, *Boy indoor plumbing really rocks!* I never drive to work appreciating how wonderful a material concrete is to drive on.

These things aren't making me any happier even though they're making life easier. Instead, I'm feeling lazy when I'm at Amberly's gymnastics class and always feeling I need to get more involved.

Why?

I've talked about a lot of things that really have gotten easier in time. But I'm about to blow your mind, or maybe just be mildly clever. While life is easier in what we *think* are important ways, it is harder, if not impossible, in the most important way.

The Importance of Being Average

This is going to show you what really matters in your mind. And it's going to show you why we aren't any happier than our ancestors. Ready?

It is a lot harder to be special today.
And that's what really matters to us.

There's no doubt the percentage of special people in the world has diminished exponentially over the last thousand years. Before we became one giant tribe, connected by T.V., radio, and the Internet, every leader of every tribe was special. Every good musician in every small village was valued. Every fine craftsman in every little town had a niche. Every wise man, on every hill, at the edge of every little hovel was revered as someone who had something unique to offer the world. The world used to be defined by so small an area that you could actually be something different within it.

But today, you have to give up everything for even a chance at special. It's too hard. Athletes give up *decades* of their lives for the opportunity to be the best in the world for ten seconds. Musicians practice their life away hoping for one break. Writers live and die, constructing volumes that no one ever sees, hoping for *one* best seller. And college kids like me give up their youth, friends, and families, in order to put letters after their names.

Special asks for too much.

And that's why we have to do something unnatural— embrace average. I realize that embracing average is *unnatural* for us. Our caveman brains naturally seek out exceptional.

But we have constructed a very unnatural world for those caveman brains, a world that turns our natural tendencies into liabilities. If we want to function better in *this* world, we need to profoundly reexamine our relationship with ourselves.

John Grace

So join the average revolution.

Run away from special and join the revolution of the nobodies. Pack your bags. The circus is in town. And we're asking you to leave with us. Hop on board the train to nowhere. Forget that mountain in the distance; we've got endless fields of corn to see. We're going on a family trip and every time we pass a white car, a gas station, or a fast-food restaurant we're going to stop and appreciate their majesty. We're driving right by the Grand Canyon, the Statue of Liberty, and Mount Rushmore.

Special doesn't get a big seat at our table. We're going to look at all the boring things in our lives. I'm enjoying more of the folks in McDonalds. Liking more people on the streets. I'm holding more conferences with nobodies. Listening to Average Joe's opinion. I'm making sure the street-sweepers get the memo and reminding the janitor about the meeting. The lawn guy is getting more interesting and the cosmetologist has a good point. The security guard, insurance salesman, and librarian don't like getting up early. But they all manage to do it anyway. And I'm starting to pay more attention to them than Brad Pitt and Britney Spears.

Can I Please Get an Award for Being Average?

Don't drink the water. Don't breathe the air. Don't walk on the sidewalk. But don't be scared. Catch 22. We got me. We got you. We got us all. What do we do? Do we cry? Do we laugh? Do we feel? Do we groan? Average. Average. Average. Means we're not alone.

The sun is mad at me.

That's what Amberly says when the sun shines in her eyes. Right now the sun is shining in my eyes, making it hard for me to see my computer, forcing me to type slowly, disrupting my chain of thought.

That gaseous ball of flaming hydrogen is getting in the way of all of the fantastic things I'd type, if only I could see my computer better.

That's a good excuse.

Excuses are the backbone of my existence.

My computer cheats at solitaire. My scale lies. It's the maid's day off. I was gonna get that fixed. I'm getting around to that. Oh, I forgot to tell you. Late charge. Finance charge. Charge it. I lost my receipt. I voided my warranty. No one explained that to me. I didn't think I needed that.

I stumble through life constantly saying how sorry I am that I'm human. I feel like I should come with some sort of warning label.

[Caution]
[Fragile]
[Unpredictable under stress]
[Contents under pressure]
[Open at your own risk]

Then when people ask, "Hey could you help with this?"
I could respond, "You know I'm a human being right? I know I look like a sentient, capable bipod. But I'm actually human. By the looks of that job, it seems you probably want it done well. I'm not going to be able to live up that kind of outlandish expectation."

Along those lines, I'm going to start wearing more baseball caps. People expect a lot less from you when you wear a baseball cap. It's like a dunce cap for our society—I'm all about decreasing expectations.

We use a lot of excuses for ourselves when our lives turn out average. If it weren't for this, I'd be President. If it wasn't for that, I'd be rich. I dated a model once. I had a dream job but someone stole it.

In other words, we'd all be somewhere special, if only something didn't happen by mistake to make our lives average. This average existence wasn't supposed to happen to us.

We get really good at *blaming* others because our lives turned out average. Blame implies something bad happened. But if we liked average, we wouldn't blame people for making our lives average. We would thank them.

That would be a pretty funny award ceremony. Here's my thank-you speech at the First Annual Average Awards.

Thank You Speech at Average Awards.

"Hello. Hello.

The Importance of Being Average

Thank you all for coming.

Hi. How are you?

Thanks for stopping by to celebrate the fact that I took out a second mortgage. I know some of you are here in honor of my potbelly and receding hairline. Let's not forget that. We'll get to you as well.

I've gotten a lot of accolades about my outburst at the stop sign yesterday. And I guess the cat is out of the bag—I did get passed over for that promotion.

Thank you. Thanks.

Before we get to the cake and the gifts, I just want to say that an average performance like this isn't just about me. It's really about the people that have made me average.

I know that.

I know that without a lot of you out there working hard to keep me down, I wouldn't be in the place I am.

So, I'd like to thank my son for not being valedictorian.

I want to thank my boss for overlooking my exceptional qualities.

I really appreciate all the work the bank did to insure I didn't get too good of a deal on that loan.

And of course, mom and dad. You withheld all of your great athletic genes to make sure I didn't excel in sports.

And where would I be without my wife.

Thank you honey. Thank you for the nagging. Thank you for the petty arguments. Without your tireless efforts, I may have found myself in a fairy tale.

And this award isn't just about the big players. It's not just about the stars. This house was built by a lot of small bricks. There are a lot of little people out there that have worked very hard to make my life average. I don't want to forget about them.

The guy who gave me the finger on the highway last week—thank you.

The woman who cut in line at the grocery store—I appreciated that.

That gas station in Georgia that stole $13.00—you know I lov ya!

And thanks for that home shopping product that disappointed me.

These are the unsung heroes of my averageness. Without them, my life might be something special. So I just wanted to say:

Thank you rude-coffee shop man.

Thank you over-priced contractor.

Thank you poor investment advice.

It's more than people. There's a spiritual side to all of this.

Nature and fate have also played a role in my averageness. I can honestly say, without some significant intervention on this level, I would have to consider my life better than average.

So I'd be remiss if I didn't acknowledge the storm that filled my yard with debris, the bugs that ruined my lawn, and the lightning that knocked out my power just after I filled my refrigerator.

I've been blessed with an abundance of mediocrity. My cup runneth over.

Thank you. All of you.

I appreciate this award.

I've worked moderately hard at being average. I wouldn't be here without all of you making sure that I didn't get ahead of you.

And I see Mr. and Mrs. Jones out there in the audience.

That means a lot.

I owe the Joneses a special thanks for keeping up with me. They made sure I didn't get too far ahead.

They've managed to keep us together. And only together can we minimize anything that might make any of us unique.

Thank you.

Thanks again.

Enjoy the cake."

Even if you have strengths, even if you have incredible abilities, you will end up average.

I'm an average doctor. The NBA is loaded with *average* professional basketball players. My college was filled with average professors. Wherever you are in life, a professional athlete, a PhD, or homeless on the street, you will likely be average there.

The need to be special is only going to do one thing. You won't get along well with the other athletes, PhDs, or homeless because you'll have to be better than them.

I've said it before. Average is not a reality. Average is a *mentality*. Start focusing on all of the things you think are boring in your life. There just might be some amazing things hiding in there.

Start thinking average.

John Grace

The Enemies of Average

Mickey Mouse
Whitney Houston
Cinderella
Bathroom Stalls
Waiters at Fancy Restaurants
School Buses
Academia

It's time we discuss the enemies to our revolution dear friends. This may not be easy but I'm afraid it must be done because the enemies to average are everywhere. I have to show you how to fight them.

Let's start with *Mickey Mouse*. *Mickey Mouse* has gotten self-centered over the last twenty years or so. He started off as a pretty average looking mouse. But now I see him wearing all these extravagant costumes with glitter, top hats, magic wands, and badges. Mickey knows all about being special. Isn't there a *Disney* song like this?

"No matter how you're heart is grieving, if you keep on believing, the dream that you wish will come true."

Let's just start by rewriting that right now. An average version would go something like:

"No matter how your heart is feeling. If you just give up dreaming. Then dreaming won't mean as much as you."

93

Then there's Whitney Houston. She said,

"One moment in time when I'm more than I thought I could be."

One moment? One moment in a whole life? Whitney? Really?

That sucks. That isn't good enough for me. I'll be darn if I'm living out the rest of my life hoping for one dinky moment. How messed up is our world when we're giving up everything for *one moment*?

What is that saying? What is that message? I'll tell you what that song means. It means that average sucks so bad that you should give up everything you can, for one moment of not being average. It is the antithesis of this book. I say take that one moment in time and buy a cheeseburger with it. Enjoy that cheeseburger. Then enjoy the fries, the shake, and the movie that you watch with all the time that you saved by not being so damn special!

Let the shades come down on this overindulgence or pretty soon we'll all be as superficial and lonely as everyone in L.A. hoping and wishing the spotlight, the beautiful glorious spotlight, will point our way for just one moment in time.

***

Unfortunately, *Cinderella* is also in on the plot. And this really hurts because Amberly and I play *Cinderella* a lot.

Yesterday Amberly was *Cinderella* and I was the Prince. Then I was the *Cinderella* and she was the prince. That was a pretty interesting sight—watching my three-year-old chase after me holding my ragged size-twelve-sandal saying, "Come back my love, come back! Here is your slipper."

I have to admit it was nice to feel like a princess. But make no mistake—*Cinderella* hates average. She could have married some average guy like the rest of us. But no-o-o. She *had* to marry the prince.

I guess as long as there has been fairy tales people have been ignoring average.

***

Even our bathroom stalls hate average these days. I was in the commode at an office building and I noticed that the walls of stall were made of particleboard that was painted to look like marble stone. We've gotten so *stuck* on ourselves that we need to be surrounded by marble when we use the toilet. Even if we can't really afford marble stone, we need to have the illusion of marble for our bowels to function.

Tell those marble stalls to take a hike. Run to port-o-potties! Seek out poorly constructed toilets. Walk away scoffing from bathroom attendants. Do we really need someone there to put soap in our hands?

Or let's beat them at their own game. Let's show them what a pain all of this narcissism is. Get your own personal, monogrammed attaché' case and carry your own private roll of toilet paper, a sterilized towel, and your own personalized brand of scented lotion into the bathroom with you.

When the bathroom attendant says, "Towel sir?"

Roll your eyes and say, "My goodness no! I have brought my own. And I will not be partaking of your communal gum either." Then you can mutter some disgraceful term like "Savage" or "Brute" under your breath.

***

School buses also hate average. I just saw the latest flagship of the maize fleet strut proudly into my subdivision last Tuesday. It didn't even vaguely resemble the school buses from my childhood. It had sleek, modern lines. Rich, dark, tinted windows. The tires were new and shiny. The chrome was bright and polished. It looked like it should be driven by *The Terminator* rather than the guy they had driving it.

Do you see what we're up against? This battle against special is going to be hard if we have to go toe-to-toe with every school bus in the country.

The war against being unique, this epic struggle between mediocrity and the pinnacle of human achievement is going to take every ounce of strength from every fiber of our being.

***

The academic world is also our enemy. They hate average in academia. There is nothing more special in academia than to publish a book or article. People sit around in dinner jackets, sipping tea, and speaking fine English, so they can ask each other about their latest successes and failures at publishing things.

For those like me, average folk who don't publish anything, it can be an embarrassing reminder of how average we are.

"Are you published?"

"What are you publishing now?"

"It's publish or perish you know?"

"When are you going to get that published?"

"You should try and get that published?"

The Importance of Being Average

But now that I've accepted average, now that I'm surfing this wave of anonymity, this whole publish thing rolls off my back like water off a duck.

Now when they ask, "Well Dr. Grace, are you published?"

I can respond with, "No. I'm stupid. That's why I'm not published. I'm stupid and I'm proud of it."

"Oh well Dr. Grace. Don't you think you're being a little hard on yourself?"

"No. No. You don't get it. I'm not ashamed of it. I was just answering your question. The reason I'm not published is that I'm not smart enough to think of anything worth publishing."

"Oh...oh...oh well. Maybe you'll publish something soon?"

"No. No. Probably not. I don't plan on getting any smarter in the coming years. And I've pretty much decided to stop trying.

I feel comfortable with the stability of my stupidity. It's not going anywhere. You can depend on me being dumb for some time.

If I publish anything I'll have to publish it myself."

"Oh well. Well good luck with that then."

"And good luck to you as well. Being smart and all."

***

Join me my friends in our war against the powers of spectacular. Chant in unison a creed against the superlative.

"Oh Narcissists of the World. Hear us.

Let go. Put down your earthly trappings.

Forget your perfect noses! Walk the fine line of commonality. Repent. Repent we say. And breathe deep into the waters of the nobody.

Repent.

But don't repent for your soul. Relinquish your special ways because it is a funnier way to live your life and a heck of a lot easier.

Dance like a fool! Sing like an idiot! Do your taxes like a caveman! Drive like a teenager! Stop trying to find a better way. That's too hard."

We're not leaving. And every day more and more of the special people are joining our ranks. Just look at how many people who used to be special are now average. Think of all of the celebrities who fall *out* of the spotlight. We even have reality television shows for celebrities who used to be famous but are now average again.

They can run from us. But they can't hide. They all end up average.

Or *maybe*, we'll all end up special? That's a *scary* thought. Could that be possible? Is the average human being in danger of going extinct? Should we call Greenpeace? Are the average man and woman endangered?

Marketers *do* hunt them mercilessly. Advertisers fire at them whenever they see average people without name-brand shoes and designer jeans. They rush to convert them to one of the elite. Andy Warhol said that in the future everyone would be famous for fifteen minutes. Perhaps Andy was saying that soon there wasn't going to be any average people left?

That frightens me. I like the gas station attendant. I love the employees at *McDonalds*. I enjoy the video store guy. Our postman is cool. And there is this quirky guy at Wal-Mart that cracks Amberly up. It makes me sad to think that soon they may be gone—hunted to extinction by dreams of being something spectacular.

We need to save *Homo Sapien Averagecus*! We need to start a sanctuary for the specially challenged.

That's it. That's it! Now we have it.

The Importance of Being Average

We're going to make being average a disability! We'll lobby congress and get protection under the American's with Disability Act.

Then none of us can get fired for being average. None of us can be discriminated against for being average. And we can get really upset if police profile us or search our cars because they said we were average.

John Grace

Sing in the Middle of McDonald's

Amberly is dancing in the middle of *McDonald's* right now. I'd like to tell you that Amberly is the most graceful dancer but right now she's dancing more like Elaine from *Seinfeld* than a ballerina.

She's a klutzy, clunky kid. When I watch her dance, when I watch her trip, when I watch her stumble, I *know* my average kid is going to struggle in this world.

The world is hard. It's very tricky. I'm only an average man trying to prepare her for it. And I'm not going to do an amazing job of that. I'm not that great of a dancer. So why should she need to be? She's probably going to make it in life about as well as she makes it on the dance floor: a lot of trips, some bruises, and some tears. Her dance in life is going to be a million miles short of *Swan Lake*.

Keep dancing like a fool Amberly. Daddy will always be smiling—even when you trip. Tripping is *part* of the dance.

There is a lady singing in the booth next to me. She is softly singing with the jukebox while Amberly dances. At first, I thought it was annoying but now I'm really listening. She's out of tune. Her voice is soft—she doesn't sound as melodic as the record.

But it's a *human* voice, not a recording and there is real human emotion behind it. And suddenly I like her song *better* than the juke box.

We're going to find more and more ways to do things better than we can. Modern sound studios make music better than people can play. Robots make cars faster. Assembly lines build sturdier furniture. The more we look around, the more we see how pathetic we are at doing most things. It gets easier and easier to be ashamed of ourselves.

But I love that pathetic daughter of mine. And I want her to be proud of being a human being even though it means being proud of being pathetic.

I think we told ourselves a long time ago that we were going to make all of these things better so that we could spend more time liking each other. We were going to build cars on assembly lines so that we could spend more time playing football in the yard. We were going to produce all of the music in one city so that the rest of us could spend our time dancing.

But we're not dancing and we're not relaxing. Instead we're all looking to be head of the factory making cars and tripping over each other to be on *American Idol*. We all want to be the *one* person making music rather than the five billion people dancing to it. It's more fun to dance. If we could just enjoy being average, we'd dance more.

I'm trying to dance more and show my daughter how to dance. I'm trying to enjoy real people singing out of tune more than synthesized perfection.

An Average Apology

Part of this journey is realizing that a lot of people had life figured out better than I did. My discovering average isn't like Columbus landing on the shores of Virginia. It's more like being fashionably late to a Christmas Party—people were already here having cocktails when I showed up.

I see the wisdom of those people now. But rather than resent them for it, I'm just thankful I figured it out in time to appreciate a clumsy dance in *McDonalds*. Part of liking average is forgiving myself for taking a long time to figure it out—it also means accepting I'll *never* figure it all out.

I'm sorry for trying. One nice thing about accepting average is that it gets easier to say you're sorry. You accept that you're a screw-up. You accept you're likely to make a lot of mistakes. You get very good at apologizing.

Like every other average person on this planet, I know I've hurt a lot of people along the way. But I'm not sorry because I'm ashamed. With what I had to work with, I was destined to hurt a fair amount of people. I'm sorry because I hurt them. And I'm saying I'm sorry because I want them to feel better.

When you need to be special you say you're sorry because you're ashamed that you aren't being special—you say you're sorry to punish yourself.

But when you're okay being average it's not about you. You say your sorry to help the people you've hurt. Those are the apologies that mean the most. I'm not apologizing because *I* want to feel better. I'm apologizing because I want *you* to feel better.

So to those of you out there—you know who you are—I'm sorry.

***

Boy it's a nice night. I wish Dad were here. I wish Dad could hold Amberly. If my world were perfect, if my world was special, he would be here. But he isn't. I have an average life with some miracles and some tragedy. If I focus on the tragedy, I'll miss the miracles.

My little girl is here now—sleeping in her room. I have to take whatever life gives me and soak it up like a sponge because life never gives average people too much happiness for long.

I walk into Amberly's room and lay next to her as she sleeps. My hand brushes her hair. And I remember my mother brushing my hair as a child. I remember my father whispering, "I love you." I remember all of the average people who have been kind to me in life, who have sacrificed for me. I realize I'm a decent human being because a lot of people took a little time to care. They're here with me as I brush Amberly's hair.

They're inside of me, flowing through me—all of the average goodness that has touched me in a lifetime. I watch in awe as a hundred pairs of hands softly caress my daughter's hair as she sleeps. Thank you. All of you. Thank you for teaching me how to love my little girl. I finally get it. I finally appreciate you. I hear all of you. I hear a thousand decent voices echo every time my daughter says, "I love you, Daddy."

My precious beautiful, little girl is built with small pieces of average love handed down through a thousand years. Every person who was kind to my great, great grandfather helped me to love my little girl. And my voice will one day join a chorus that sings, "We love you." To all of tomorrow's children.

The Importance of Being Average

Each of us is a nameless, faceless singer in a song that will echo through the stars long after our children's children pass on. Our actions matter. Our kindness matters. Our lives matter even though they are not remembered.

Being average means being forgotten.

Appreciating average means appreciating that even forgotten people make a difference.

John Grace

Curse of the Pink Air Tank

I just tripped over a comic book of *Daffy Duck* in the living room.

I had a large comic book collection when I was a kid. I used to enjoy reading them but then I got too *serious* about collecting. For the last twenty years I've carried around twenty-three boxes of comic books, monitored their value in the latest price guides, maintained their pristine condition so I could worship them inside plastic bags—I've stressfully followed each swing in the comic market.

It's been a long time since I *enjoyed* reading *any* of them. Comic books, baseball cards, stamps and even rocks aren't collected anymore. They're worshiped. Stuck in bags without any air. Never read. Never picked up. Never enjoyed. Everyone is so afraid of making them average.

So, the comic book of superman #1 is worth more never read. Even though that means it's never *really* been enjoyed.

Isn't a comic book that a kid never reads really a waste? Shouldn't the baseball card that has never been in somebody's back pocket be the worthless one? Isn't the best thing about collecting the connection to a child's world? I need to stop worshiping the best things in my life and start enjoying them.

Speaking of my life…it's in chaos. My house is a mess. My furniture is all over my lawn. We had the floors cleaned and now everything is outside. And I have to get it back inside.

I keep screwing things up as I'm trying to bring big pieces of furniture in the door. And while I'm doing all of this and looking like a complete idiot, I take a look at the T.V. There is a televangelist speaking to her congregation. She tells them that the power of God is flowing through her. She can heal all of their illnesses.

While she's trying to heal *a thousand* people at once, I'm trying to get this damn couch to fit through a door that it went through twelve hours ago.

I switch the channel. Next thing I get is *Cops*. And I see some poor drunk sap having a really bad night. I look at him and I look at all of the furniture on my lawn. Then I start wondering if I'm breaking some sort of law by having all of the contents of my house in my yard. I couldn't live like this forever—there must be some *law* against living on your lawn.

That makes me nervous. Police officers are another one of those oxy-moron things like insurance. Cops are supposed to make us feel *safe* but all I ever think when I see them is, *Oh boy, I hope I'm not screwing up.* Like right now. I'm hoping a cop doesn't come by and write me a ticket for having my house on my lawn. I wonder if the ACLU would fight for my right to live in my yard?

***

Getting my house off my lawn is just one of my recent problems. This morning I stopped at *Dunkin' Donuts* for a quick coffee.

It ended up spilled on my computer.

I lost some of my book. Wouldn't you know it—I think they were the most amazing pages ever written.

When I say that I screw things up, when I say I miss things, when I say that I let things slip, I mean *big* things. I mean big chunks of time. I mean risky things like homeowners insurance and safety checks on my tires. My life is a series of large screw-ups with small victories interspersed just frequently enough that I get the crazy notion that I may one day pull it all together.

Coffee all over my computer. A month's worth of work lost because I was too lazy to back it up. What's wrong with me? I'm not stupid—I'm incompetent.

That's funny because as a psychiatrist I work for the county and help to declare people incompetent when they are no longer able to manage their affairs.

If I look down the list of things required for competence:

Able to manage bills.
Able to manage medications.
Able to manage appointments.
Able to drink a cup of coffee without ruining a $600.00 computer.

Okay, maybe that last one isn't there but if I'm really honest about that list, I'm only competent four days a week. I don't think any of us are competent *all* of the time. If I were playing on a sport team in life, they would have benched me a long time ago.

And to make it worse, I've been carrying around a big, pink, helium tank in my car for the last seven months. We bought it for Amberly's birthday party—now I can't get rid of the damn thing.

Garbage men won't take it. City dump told me to take a hike. Every day I get into the car I have this big pink air tank riding shotgun—mocking me.

I don't have any money. I don't know where my wallet is. My computer is fried. My furniture is on my lawn. And I have a big, pink, helium tank laughing at me wherever I go. I swear if you would have asked me how I was doing thirty hours ago, I would have told you pretty good.

I should have known better. Maybe I should eat a pound of chocolate. Game over. I'm going to sleep on the floor for a few hours. I want to sleep on my bed—too bad it's in the front yard.

I don't judge people harshly for struggling because I know how hard it is to lead an average life today. The whole thing is an artificial bubble. We are all breathing on a respirator. None of us knows what it feels like to live as a real human being.

We wear clothes so they don't see us naked. We wear antiperspirant so they don't see us sweat. We wear cologne so they don't smell us. We read books so they understand us. We get alarms because we're late. We get maps because we're lost. We get an education so we're not stupid. We get plastic surgery so we look better. We get money so they know we're important.

And despite all of these extraordinary efforts our lives tumble into average and we end up riding in cars with pink air tanks laughing at us.

An Average Piano Player Worth a Thousand Dollars an Hour

This is the story of a piano player who changed my life while I was at a medical conference.

They have names for groups of things: a flock of sheep, a murder of crows, and a gaggle of geese. What do you call a group of psychiatrists? A Freud? Yeah. Maybe.

So I was at a conference with a Freud of Psychiatrists and there were a lot of people making a lot of money talking about medications.

It was boring. Not because the material was boring but because I didn't know anyone. It's lonely to go to conferences because no one talks to anyone, except for maybe in the bar after the day is over.

Between meetings, Courtney, Amberly and I went to the mall. It was a fancy mall. I went from feeling like a nobody at the conference to feeling like a nobody at the mall.

Amberly went on a kid's train ride. The ride lasted four minutes. There were six or seven other kids on the train with her. Amberly tried to talk to them, tried to play with them, but the other parents discouraged it. So we discouraged it.

And I saw a *change* in my daughter's eyes. It was the first time Amberly learned it *wasn't* okay to play with every kid she met.

We left the train and continued browsing the mall. Most people wore expensive clothes. They wanted you to look at them but not stare too long. I shook my head.

We heard a piano and were drawn into the main foyer. There was a giant fountain shooting water forty feet in the air. It was a pretty special fountain. Near the fountain was a middle-age man in a tuxedo playing a gorgeous black grand piano. I'm not a connoisseur but he was the best pianist I've ever heard. He seemed friendly. His eyes were kind. He smiled as Amberly and I approached. I held her up and allowed her to see the inner workings of his piano. He started playing *Twinkle Twinkle Little Star.*

Amberly started singing to him.

It was a wonderful moment in my life. But it was bitter sweet. I realized this piano player who got paid $10/hour was enriching my life more than the professors getting paid more than a $1000/hour over at the conference. It's too bad that we don't reward the people that touch us the most.

Average people do more for me on a day-to-day basis than special people. I walk by them most of the time. I'm too busy looking for special people or too focused on trying to make myself special.

But I'm trying to learn to stop and appreciate them. I appreciated the piano player. I wanted to sit with him. I wanted to have dinner with him and thank him for the beautiful gift he gave my daughter. I wanted to hear his story.

The world doesn't allow us to meet strangers any more. "Stranger" doesn't mean the same as it used to. It used to be someone you didn't know. Now it's someone you don't *want* to know. We're not interested in meeting most strangers. Strangers are most likely average—why would we want to have anything to do with them?

But when you realize *you're* average. You realize you're a stranger to the rest of the world. Suddenly you have a little more compassion for people you don't know.

Amberly and I walked away from the piano player. All we shared was a smile.

It bothered me to think of the world my daughter was growing up in. It wasn't because of the violence or poverty. It wasn't education and it wasn't inequality. I wasn't sad because my daughter was growing up in troubled times, times have always been troubled.

I was sad because she was going through life alone. For all the people that were in that mall, none of them cared about Amberly. None of those kids would play with her. She would never talk to that piano player. She would stay away from strangers the rest of her life. And she would be a stranger to most of the world. That meant the world would stay away from her.

Our world is smaller than it's ever been but lonelier too. Aborigines in a tribe of three hundred in The Outback have more intimate contacts than Manhattan socialites who live within a block of a million people. Our children have fewer people they are close to than any time in the history of human beings. They have more contact with people and ideas through television, music, and the Internet—but less intimacy. That makes them more alone.

That's the biggest crime of seeking special—intimacy terrifies you. And you run from it. You isolate and pull away from everyone. As our world has begun to care more about special than average, it's stopped caring about *most* of the people in the world. The world stopped caring about my average little girl.

I'm not talking about somebody in the middle of Montana sending Amberly a birthday card—I don't expect that. But the neighbor's kids take more interest in *MTV*, *Teen Magazine,* and Paris Hilton than Amberly. Special people and special places have stolen every drop affection and attention that belongs in our average, little neighborhoods. The spotlights shine so brightly in L.A. that the rest of us are living in darkness.

My daughter deserves the love of her neighbors. She deserves their affection. She needs their warmth and validation. But it's been stolen by special. It's lost. We worship Mary Kate and Ashley from our televisions rather than notice the average boys and girls trying to grow up in our little towns. And eventually, kids think they need to be worshiped in order to be worth anything—so most of them end up disgusted with themselves for failing at becoming icons.

I don't want that for my little girl. She shouldn't hate herself because she can't make it on the cover of a magazine.

I don't need the whole planet to look at Amberly. I just need a few people to love average enough to take an interest in her. She needs that so that she can have a little satisfaction when she ends up making $10.00/ hour. She needs that to have a little self-respect when she wears a size-eight dress.

***

We have a *right* to privacy in our country. We have privacy *laws*. We don't let people know *our* business. Somewhere along the way, we all got the idea that *isolation* is a *great* idea. We live in a self-imposed prison of insecurity because we're afraid of being cast away, and march ourselves to Elba, choosing self-exile over self-disclosure—because we would rather run away from the world while saying we're special than stay within it and admit we're average. If you *have* to be special, you will spend the rest of your life trying to hide the fact beneath it all—you *really* are average.

The Importance of Being Average

I see a lot of different strata in my office. People share more than they imagine. Most of us could be friends if we could accept and share the average parts of our lives: our fears, failures, and minor victories. For most of us, those are the *same* things.

When people are *forced* to get along, they discover that. That's one nice thing about having family close, or living in a small town, or being on *Survivor* for that matter. You are forced to have relationships with people—that means you're forced to accept them. You're forced to forgive them and tolerate average, imperfect relationships.

That's the only way humans form relationships. Otherwise, sooner or later, everyone lets us down. Then we run away, certain that out there—somewhere—is an *ideal* relationship. So we give up on our friends and go look for better people to hang out with...but we never find them.

But when we finally love average, we stop looking for *special* people to have relationships with and start improving the average relationships right in front of us.

This book is my effort at breaking the ice and being more intimate with a lot of strangers. This is who I am. These are some of the things I think about. Come talk to me and appreciate my average daughter.

***

I can't spend too much time being bitter—then I miss average myself. I miss the *whole* point. If I'm too angry about the world not caring about my daughter, I forget to see how *beautiful* she is while she is being ignored.

The fact of the matter is...Amberly smiled while she was on that train...she smiled as we walked away from the pianist.

Amberly smiled…while the world ignored her. She made the best of being forgotten.

I'd never seen somebody so beautiful while being ignored. Looking at her, looking at that average magnificent smile, made me forget about the people ignoring her, other than to feel sorry for them for what they were missing.

The world is probably going to ignore Amberly. But that's the world's problem—not hers. I hope she keeps smiling while it ignores her. I hope she finds people wise enough to appreciate average because they will appreciate her smile.

I'm proud of you Amberly. You have no idea how many people you've helped in life. Every person in my office has been helped by you. I became a better man and a better doctor from the first day you were in my life. The pressure is off. Your life is already a success.

So enjoy it. I'm trying to teach you how. I'm trying to enjoy my average life and love the average part of myself because *that's* what I want you to do. I want you to be like me. I want you to love your insecurities, your frailties. I want you to love the things you do badly as much as the things you do well.

It wasn't easy to learn how to love the worst parts about myself—the world didn't make that easy. But I knew the only way I could *teach* you was to show you. This story is the story of an average man learning to love an average life for the sake of preparing his average children for an average future.

Amberly, I would give my life to make sure your life turns out special. That isn't in my power. The best I have for you is to help you enjoy average. Smile little girl. Smile while you struggle and you'll smile frequently. And I'll be smiling with you.

Thank you for saving *me* with your smile.

You never know *when* you're going to make a difference in someone's life. Usually it isn't something amazing you do that *makes* a difference. Usually it's the little things, the average things that happen by chance to be done at *just* the right time to have an amazing impact. Average at the right moment can save the world.

But you have to enough faith to believe. Being average requires faith. If all you can expect from yourself is a mediocre performance then you're going to need a lot of help to get anything done.

But you'll *get* that help sometimes and just might do unbelievable things with average actions—like when an average four-year-old girl helped change a thousand lives by smiling at her father.

John Grace

PART III

BEING AVERAGE

For the second time in my life, my daughter's smile saved me. She first taught me to love average that day in the pool. Then she showed me how to let it go. And she did it with simple beauty—a child's smile.

My average, little girl was so beautiful in that moment that I didn't have room in my perception for anything but love. There wasn't room for special. There wasn't room for anger. There wasn't room for fear.

For the first time I looked at my daughter and I *wasn't* afraid for her. I didn't *worry* about her. I wasn't *angry* at the world for hurting her.

I wasn't angry I couldn't save average. I was grateful. Grateful that I could look at her and see her as she truly was— average. An average human being who magnificently tried to make the world brighter even while it ignored her.

I didn't need to save her anymore. I didn't need to save average. I didn't need a soapbox, pedestal, or crusade. Average was going to be just fine. In fact, average saved me.

I stepped back and saw things clearly. I appreciated being average.

Enjoy *The Importance of Being Average. Part III: Being Average.*

Don't forget to laugh. Don't forget to cry.

Don't forget to love.

Loving is the best way to be average.

John Grace

An Average Doctor's Life's Work

We're nearly finished with our journey into the deep recesses of my bland existence. I feel like a white sheet is enveloping each piece of my mind, covering all the little jagged edges, so that an amorphous blob is all that is left with smooth corners, and cushions. And all of those sharp, little pieces of special are being overrun by a giant Jell-O bubble. I am becoming a soft pile of goop, warm and fuzzy—harder to define but easier to love.

We all love fuzzy. Think about all of our favorite childhood toys. Stuffed animals. Silly putty. Jell-O. We are drawn to blobs. We are innately in love with blurry shapes. We are born to love average. Only in time do we stamp out the warm and fuzzy figures of our life to replace a cuddly bear with a strong, clearly defined army soldier.

The journey into average is really a journey into a blob. It is about letting go of the need to separate, crystallize, and contrast. Wrap yourself in a warm cushy blanket. I want to be a blob to my friends, a gushy lump that they love, hold and hug but are completely unimpressed with.

On we glide, fellow Jell-O members. I'm using my spare tire and love handles to full advantage. Another great thing about this party is that you can invite as many people as you want. There's no velvet rope. There's no cover charge. There's no paparazzi. They are all over at the special party.

So come on in. Have a glass of wine. Dance as bad as you want to. I guarantee we'll have more fun than they do because we aren't afraid of looking like idiots. In fact, we relish in it.

Human beings have an innate, exceptional ability to look foolish. Trust in this ability. Believe in yourself. I believe in you. I believe in your ability to screw up most things that you try. That is why I extend you an invitation to the average party.

I went into medicine to do something amazing, to help thousands of people and change lives. But now I'd be satisfied if I could just help a few of them. I don't need save any villages. If I can make a small, average group of people smile, if I can make life better for a few days for the people who have done everything for me, then it was all worth it.

This is the most important work of my life. And it's nothing. Two hundred smiles make up a life. And if you can help two hundred people smile for a day then you have given enough. That's all I hope to do with this. And that's all I hope to do with my life.

This is the best I have to give. This book. It is my training. It is my heart. It is my love. And it is given as a way of thanking the small group of people who never appreciated themselves as much as they should have because I never appreciated them as much as I should have. I may not be able to help those closest to me in my office, but maybe I can help them a little in here.

So to the people who know me, who really know me, please take this book for what it really is. It's a piece of my heart, a piece of my mind, and a piece of my love. Let it make you smile.

Appreciating the Average Beauty Closest to Me

I used to do a radio show once a week where I talked about mental health issues. Before you start thinking that makes me a celebrity, you need to understand that I paid the radio station to do the show and no one ever recognized me.

I almost got recognized once. I called someone's house to ask for donations for a local charity. "Hello this is Dr. Grace. Is Sandy Wilson home?" I was calling to speak to Sandy because I wanted to ask her about a possible donation."

"Dr. Grace? Dr. John Grace?" she asked.

A spark went off in my mind. *I'm finally going to be recognized. Someone must know me from the show. This is it! I'm going to be special.*

"Why yes. Yes. It is Dr. Grace." I answered proudly.

"This is Sandy. Don't you remember me we used to work together a few years ago?" The woman answered.

My heart sunk. It turned out that I wasn't recognized from the radio. I was recognized from my life. That's the average way to get recognition. It burst my bubble at the time. I'm okay with it now.

Try to get recognized for the average part of your life.

***

Two friends of mine, Larry and Robyn co-hosted the radio show with me. Larry and Robyn are also writers. Their books taught me a valuable lesson about appreciating average art and literature.

Larry had shown me several of his books in the past. I hadn't got around to reading them. And I was thinking about why I hadn't read them as we were talking one day—the truth was—I didn't think they were good enough to read.

They'd never been on the *New York Times Best Seller List*. I'd never seen them on the television, in any supermarkets, or bookstores. The critics never *told* me to read them. My impression was they were just average, children's books that had never succeeded at climbing to the top of the heap.

I also remember thinking one time it would be neat if Larry and Robin's books caught on because then I would know two famous authors. I would surely read their books if that happened—if some stranger from the *Washington Post* told me to.

I've learned since then.

While writing this book, I bought Larry's and Robyn's books—all of them. And I read them to Amberly. But I didn't read them like they were books that failed to be on the *New York Times Best Seller's List*. I didn't read them like they *failed* at anything. I read them like they were written for my little girl. I read them like they were average stories. I imagined Larry and Robyn putting their hearts into those books, specifically for my child.

It felt so good to read a book from someone who gave everything to make my child smile. I imagined Larry and Robyn paying attention to every detail—reading aloud to my daughter. They were in the pages giving pieces of their life to make life a little easier for Amberly.

Average always gives more than special. Average gives *everything* it has. We always appreciate it less. I'm not doing that anymore.

The Importance of Being Average

That is what this book is about—realizing how much the average people in my life have given, taking it, and giving back to them. Thank you Larry. Thank you Robyn. Thank you for writing an average book for my average little girl. This average book was written for you.

And the truth is your book gave more love than any book from a stranger ever could have. Life means so much more when we actually touch the people that are close enough to touch. We have lost the context of most of the stories we read. We read too many stories from people we don't know. We don't appreciate the art that is closest to us—we look for art that is far away. We're afraid of a personal connection.

Start looking at the average art, stories and poetry that come into your life. Let go of Oprah's book club enough to pick up that cute little book your grandma wrote.

Write a book for your family. Paint a picture for your friends. This is my book for my family and friends. This book isn't telling you how to live your life. It's showing you.

Don't read what I do. Do what I do.

***

I took my daughter back to Chicago recently. That's where I'm originally from but we moved to Tampa eight years ago.

My love for being average put a new spin on some old things. My cousin Laura had written a song for her mother during that visit and I listened to that song just like I'd read Larry and Robyn's books.

It wasn't *U2* or *Matchbox 20.*

It was better.

And I cried a little as I listened to it because I realized I'd spent too much of my life listening to top twenty billboard hits.

***

I was at a party on that trip and I watched my family play with my daughter. I had always appreciated the fact that Amberly might someday find the *right* school. I'd always hoped that one day she might find the *right* kind of people to associate with. But I'd always overlooked the people that she didn't need to find—her family. There were a handful of people that would happily give their lives for her safety without thinking twice.

I had gone nearly thirty years and never appreciated all of the people willing to give their lives for me. I had been too busy trying to impress the other five billion people that couldn't care less. And I'd never been more ashamed of not appreciating average than when I looked at my family.

How many times do we ask for the tiniest recognition from strangers, ignoring the greatest sacrifices from those closest to us?

***

Amberly provided the laughs for the trip back from Chicago. In the airport terminal she got into a shouting match with the sun because she didn't want to put on a diaper. It was too early.

She's a big girl now and only wears diapers at nighttime. But I thought it might be a good idea if she slept on the plane.

"Hey daddy! What's the sun say? Does the sun say I have to wear a diaper?" Amberly asked.

Before I could answer she started shouting toward the air.

"Hey Sun! SUN! SUN! I don't have to wear diaper while you're out? SUN! SUN? SUN? Are you there? I only wear a diaper at night!"

I pretended like I was the sun and responded in a deep voice, "Well Amberly maybe this one time you should wear a diaper."

"NO! NO! NO! SUN! NO! I thought you were my friend. I thought you were my friend. No sun. No-o-o." Amberly then ran to the terminal windows, screaming at the glass toward a setting sun that she felt betrayed her. The airport gate had a hundred passengers watching my daughter have a shouting match with the sun.

It didn't get any better.

I had to go to the washroom. Of course, Amberly had to come as well. She chose this inopportune time to take her first interest in the difference between male and female anatomy.

We came out of the washroom with Amberly shouting to the airport terminal, "Hey, Daddy! You've got a *tail*! You've got a tail like a mermaid! Daddy, why do you have a tail? Hey everyone, my Daddy is a mermaid!"

I'm sure we gave them a good laugh. There are a thousand Amberly stories I'd like to share but I'll leave you to discover the stories of your life.

My stories aren't going to be as good as yours. They shouldn't be. That's the point.

***

On the plane Amberly pointed to my head and said, "Daddy, is your brain in there?"

"Yes, Amberly. My brain is in there." I responded.

"What's it doing in there?"

"It's just sitting."

"Is your heart in there?" She pointed to my chest.

"Yes, Amberly."

"What's it doing in there?"

"It's beating."

Amberly looked at a bowl of strawberries she had in front of her.

"Daddy, does your brain smell strawberries?"

I thought about her question. Over a lifetime, I hadn't smelled any strawberries. I'd spent a lot of time doing a lot of things but smelling things wasn't one of them. I always considered it a waste of time.

I smiled as I told her, "It does now sweetie."

"Do you want to smell my strawberries?"

"Yes. I do."

She held the bowl up to my nose and I took a deep breath. It was the first time I'd ever smelled strawberries.

A Bad Day With A Great Ending

When I got back from my trip to Chicago, I had one of the worst mornings of my life.

I was trying to mail a box to my mother. I went to the post office and waited in line for thirty minutes. Then I needed a different box. Then I had the wrong envelope. Then I couldn't get insurance. Then I needed different tape. Then I wrote the wrong address.

I ended up walking out of the post-office two hours later after spending twenty dollars on boxes and tape that I didn't use. I never even mailed the box. It was one of the more frustrating days of my life.

I called my father, nearly in tears, "What am I dad, a moron? I can't mail a stupid box in two hours with twenty dollars? What's wrong with me? My day is ruined! What should I do? I can't go do work like this!"

He laughed and said, "You should take your kid swimming."

"Yeah thanks." I hung up with him.

I was driving in the car worrying about getting everything done and I said to myself, *Hey John. Take it easy, man. It's just a box.*

I mean when life is said and done what are you really going to regret, a box?

No. What is it then? What are you going to really regret?

And I realized that my biggest regret in life was going to be that I spent too much time worrying about things that I couldn't control.

It made me smile because I realized that there was a word for letting go of things that you can't control—faith.

My biggest regret in life was going to be not having enough faith.

So I started to believe a little more. When you embrace average it's a lot easier to believe. Embracing average means letting go of the expectation we're perfect. It gets easier to see there is something worthwhile in imperfect human beings.

There *is* something good in us. I'm convinced of it. I've seen it. I've seen it in our children. I've seen it in our elderly. I've seen it when people who have never been given any decency or kindness become generous and thoughtful. If that doesn't give you faith, I don't know what does.

So with a little more faith, I took dad's advice. I took my daughter swimming, kissed my wife—made waffles. I enjoyed the things I had, the average things. It was one of the best days of my life. It was an average day after all. The postage nightmare and frustrating lines didn't hold a candle to the average stuff.

Thanks Dad.

Human beings have a limited ability to improve their lives and an unlimited ability to destroy them. Embracing average means accepting that.

It means having *faith* it will get better and not making it worse in the meantime.

***

The Importance of Being Average

I need to start wrapping up this journey. It's been a fun ride. I've learned a lot. I learned to see average and I learned to appreciate it.

A lot of people have tried to welcome me into average. A lot of people have said, "Take a load off. Stay awhile. Enjoy life."

But I always kept walking, thinking there was somewhere better to go. When I finally stopped, when I finally looked around, I realized there wasn't anywhere better.

It took a long time to like average but I see a lot of it in my life as I look back. I wish I enjoyed more of it. Better late than never. Thank God I got to appreciate being an average parent, because it's better than being special at anything else.

The sun is going to shine tomorrow. The sky is going to be blue. People are going to get up and go about their lives. And my life will go on. It sounds like it's going to be an average day.

That's my favorite kind.

I wonder if Amberly will read this book when she's old and gray and I'm long gone. I wonder if she'll hear these words after I've done the most average thing in life, which is to die.

I once wanted to write a book so that my thoughts would continue after I was gone. I was convinced if I wrote an epic, I would live forever. There's immortality in words remembered. Nothing is as special as immortality.

But I don't *need* that anymore. I don't need to live forever. I'm not even sure I'd want to. This book wasn't written for posterity. It wasn't written for dusty archives. After the people are gone who are meant to be touched by this book then this book *should* be forgotten and a new one written.

I hope Amberly writes a new one for the people in *her* life. I hope we all do. I hope this book becomes one quiet little voice in the chorus of life. I hope I sing one pleasant note of love in the background a thousand years from now, just like everyone alive today who has done anything for anyone else.

I only hope, I only dream that this book brings my children warmth in the years to come. Rather than be special, rather than change the world, this book has a more average goal. It doesn't have to sit in some library a hundred years from now, as long as it warms a little girl's heart for a lifetime.

I love you Amberly. I love you Johnny. I love you Courtney. I love you mom. I love you dad. Thank you for being average. I hope this book allows me to hold your hands for the time we share. I hope you smile when you think of it and think of me.

I set out to be someone amazing. I set out to be someone different. I set out to be someone special.

I failed.

Thank God.

Because in my failure I finally appreciated everything I am. This is who I am. That is what I accomplished. This is all I need.

All I ever needed...was average.

And now that we're all on the same page, I understand the importance of being average.

The Importance of Being Average

John Grace

Appendix One

The Scientific Theory of Appreciating Average

The Importance of Being Average is based on a simple premise:

The human mind is poorly prepared for the world we have constructed.

Civilization is a recent phenomenon dating a few thousand years. For a million years, mankind lived in a different environment...a harsher environment without the luxury of running water or light bulbs. But convenience comes with a price. Sometimes our water runs through lead pipes and our light bulbs disrupt our circadian rhythms. Our world wasn't planned with our bodies in mind.

For example, starvation was a major problem for our ancestors but in modern society *obesity* is a much bigger problem—no pun intended. People die of strokes, heart attacks and high blood pressure because our bodies are *designed* to store energy well. It isn't that we have poor discipline. We have too much food. The human body is built to live in a world in which it is starving.

Post Traumatic Stress Disorder is a disorder where an individual is exposed to a life-threatening trauma and then is overly anxious, reminded repeatedly of the trauma by even the slightest cues. Although it's a "disorder" today, it probably saved a number of our ancestor's lives.

John Grace

Imagine you're a cave woman walking along a narrow path. Suddenly, a lion attacks you. You barely escape. It serves you well to never forget that experience, to be more cautious on that path.

But if a woman is assaulted in her house today she can't avoid the cues reminding her of the attack because every Saturday she turns on the television and sees a different kind of aggression. She's overexposed to violence through the media. And an ancient impulse keeps screaming in her ear, "YOU'RE IN DANGER!" Eventually, she becomes a nervous wreck because an alarm has been triggered and she can't turn it off in our modern world.

Now what about those light bulbs?

Human beings are designed to be more active during the day. Our body temperature increases as we "warm up" in anticipation of greater activity. We perform better physically, mentally, and emotionally during the daylight hours because that is how we are *designed* to perform.

Our ancestors had clear cues when it was day and when it was night. They spent a lot of time outside, exposed to bright sunlight. A sunny day has the brightness level of 20,000-150,000 lux— a lux is a measure of brightness. Their nights were almost *total* darkness. No street lights. Just a dim fire or the soft light of the moon. At most they were exposed to a few lux at night.

But our world is *very* different. We wake in artificial light before the sun is up. We stay inside most of the day using florescent bulbs to work. These lights only provide between 100 to 500 lux. After work, most of us return home, turn on more light bulbs, and maybe watch television. We then go to bed, leaving the computer and a night light on.

In other words, most of us hang out in the 100-500 lux light range throughout the day **and** night. Most of us live our

136

lives in a perpetual dusk—we never get the natural sunlight and total darkness required to put our bodies into a rhythm.

Setting your alarm doesn't *really* wake you up. Getting in the shower doesn't wake you. Even the coffee you drink doesn't tell your body to increase it's temperature as much as the sunlight does. You *can* force your body to move. But without the sun you're body thinks it's moving at three am instead of eight am. So many people go through life in perpetual dusk...tired, irritable and never in rhythm because the world we have constructed does not produce appropriate cues to tell our bodies what time it is.

So what did our ancestors think of being average?

THEY HATED IT!
AND THEY NEEDED TO HATE IT!
HATING AVERAGE HELPED THEM TO SURVIVE.

Our ancestors lived in small tribes with anywhere from thirty to five hundred members. In a small community, it helps if people specialize, if members strive to be the *best* because there are enough jobs to go around and little overlap.

Jim should be the best at making arrows.
Sally should be the best at making clothes.
Dave should be the best at raising crops.

Everyone should *try* to be the best at whatever they're good at because the tribe needs their best. And it needs them to drive *themselves* to be the best because there is only a limited amount of competition to be the best in anything.

It's a different world today. We're a different tribe. Our "tribe" has a billion members and most of the members have no contact with each other. Instead, we are connected by the media to a few select leaders and icons. We look more like bees in a hive with a lot of workers doing redundant tasks while a small number of people make decisions. Specialization is nearly impossible, being "the best" requires beating out at least a billion people.

Imagine if every bee who was *only* a pollen harvester got depressed. You'd have a lot of depressed bees. Maybe we do?

We have a brain that tells us we need to be special because that is going to help us survive— it's going to help our tribe survive. But it's a brain that's killing us. People spend a $100,000 on a birthday party. They mortgage their future to have the best wedding cake. They go into debt so they can have a shinier car. They hurt themselves in order to feel unique. And it isn't because they're selfish. Their brain is saying that's what they *need* to do to survive because that's what our ancestors needed to do for over a million years.

Our brain tells us over and over, "BE THE BEST!" And it doesn't say it softly. It says it harshly. Mankind has a brutal relationship with himself because that's what helped our ancestors survive.

It feels more natural for human beings to hate themselves than love themselves because hating yourself helps you survive when the world is brutal.

Our ancestors needed to be very hard on themselves to survive. Our ancestors *needed* that drive. When the world hates you, you'd better hate yourself, you'd better drive yourself with near total disregard in order to make it. You can't afford to take a "mental health day" off from hunting in the Ice Age. You'll end up a well-adjusted corpse.

The Importance of Being Average

Let me give you an example how driving yourself is appropriate in one environment and disastrous in another. Jim breaks his leg. If he walks on it after two days, it will not set right. He will have a limp the rest of his life.

If Jim is a caveman one million years ago, it is the right decision to force himself to walk on that leg because if he doesn't he will starve—the world will *kill* him if he doesn't push himself. The world will kill him if he doesn't hate himself enough to not care about screwing up his leg. He needs to be cruel to himself because the world is *even* crueler.

It is appropriate for him to say to himself, *Jim, you worthless piece of garbage you HAVE to get up! I don't care about your leg! You piece of dirt! You need to go out there and hunt. Even if it kills you! GET OUT! MOVE! MOVE!*

Now. Look at a different environment...our environment. Jim is an executive—he will miss a big deal if he doesn't walk after two days. But it's the wrong decision to force himself out of bed in two days. He will not go hungry or die by taking a few weeks off. It probably is not worth walking with a limp for the rest of his life.

Do you see the point? It is appropriate to be brutal on yourself in a brutal environment. But as the world softens, so should your mind.

But what does Jim do today? Most of the time that executive will risk the limp for the deal. Not because it's the right decision but because a Neanderthal mind is making the decision. He feels like he'll die if he doesn't drive himself to walk because that's all his mind knows.

Think of how you talk to yourself. Don't most of you engage in a very harsh dialogue with yourself?

I'm so fat!
I'm so disgusting!

John Grace

I need to get this house cleaned!
If I don't finish these taxes by Friday I'll go crazy!

You talk to yourself like these are life-or-death situations. That caveman brain of yours still thinks that if you don't perform, you will die. It's driving you like the wolves are at the door. Your mind handles most of the decisions you face with too much negative emotion. That's why people kill themselves when they get fired or go crazy when they don't make the football team. Our minds were built for a deadly world that hated us. We've carried that brutality of our ancestors and continue to apply it ourselves in a way that is often counter-productive.

Even our pets do it. Think of your dog with a broken leg. He will try to stand. He will push himself to stand even when it hurts, even when you bring his food to him. Deep inside that brain is an engine that says the world will kill him if he cannot perform. He pushes himself because his ancient brain is screaming that he needs to stand even though every cue in the world today is telling him to take it easy.

That's the bad news. Now for the good news.

We can change this. We can make this world easier on our minds. And this book helps.

The purpose of this book is to show you how to be easier on yourself, to enjoy a different relationship with your world. Being "average" means being easier on yourself. It means adapting more appropriately to this softer world. Cleaning the living room shouldn't *feel* like a life-or-death struggle.

I chose humor and anecdotes to teach this. I chose modeling. That's why I chose to go on this journey myself, to show you how to do it, to show my children how to do it. It's real by the way—the journey. My tears, fears, and laughter are in these pages. This is a behind-the-curtain glimpse into changing the average human mind.

This is how to silence a voice in your head that keeps screaming,

"You're not good enough!"

A scream that began in a cave a million years ago, and echoes through all our minds today.

John Grace

Appendix Two

For Therapists

The Importance of Being Average can work as a successful adjunct with supportive psychotherapy. It is useful in modeling superego mitigation in appropriate real-world experiences.

Most of our patients are too hard on themselves, often to their own detriment. They come to us frightened and suffering, certain they are alone in their inability to negotiate the world.

This book shows them the universality of struggle and provides a road map for real change by allowing people to watch a psychotherapist conduct supportive therapy on himself. It goes through the slow process of learning to appreciate yourself despite your shortcomings.

One day a patient will ask you, "How do I learn to like myself even though I haven't done all of the things I should have?"

Hand them a copy of this book.

The Importance of Being Average uses humor and anticipation to deal with painful issues of loss and guilt in a way that we often ask of our patients. It models healthy thinking, by bringing psychotherapy away from the abstract and putting it into practice in front of a reader.

Therapists have a responsibility to not only help those struggling in the world but also aid those in a position of prominence by granting them a greater insight to the inner workings of their mind.

The human mind is destined to struggle in this world, a design flaw if you will (as discussed in appendix one) and our work transcends providing comfort to the ailing. We have a responsibility to give the world an honest appreciation of what really transpires within each of us.

The more we understand ourselves, the greater awareness we have of our potential and our potential mistakes.

At the core of this book is the idea that the human mind has retained a portion of it's vestigial harshness, the notion that we have all carried forward from our ancestors a drive to excel that is too intense to be optimal for our softer world.

There is a reason that psychotherapy helps most people. There is a reason why nearly all psychotherapy helps all conditions. And that reason is:

Nearly every mind on this planet will function better if it is a little easier on itself.

As we have changed our environment, we have had to make adjustments to help our bodies deal with a new environment.

- Anti-coagulation helps most people live longer because most of us no longer live in a world with severe cuts every day.

- Obesity is our biggest health problem because most of our bodies are "too good" at storing fat and finding food is not usually a problem.

Strong coagulation and storing fat easily were valuable traits to our ancestors. But they are liabilities for us. Wouldn't it make sense that we need to make some adjustments to our mind as well to help our caveman brains live in the 21st century?

This book is about showing people how to think better for the world today and giving them some awareness of the mind that they carry from their ancestors.

The Importance of Being Average

Appreciate the privilege you have been given to see the truth of humanity laid out before you every day. And know that I appreciate the work you do.

John Grace

Appendix Three

The Secret of Life Today

"Whoever enjoys the most average wins."

John Grace

Appendix Four

A special thanks to Kaye Coppersmith for all of her early editing advice in *The Importance of Being Average.*

This project would not be here without your help, Kaye.

You were the first person to believe in average.

John Grace

Appendix Five

The Inside Joke of My Life

ABCDEFGHIJKLMNOPQRSTUVWXYZ (In pink)

John Grace

Appendix Six

The Place for Special in the World

Just because I've become a fan of average, that doesn't mean that special doesn't have a place.

I know our movement is a big-picture, middle-of-the-road, amorphous kind of idea. But I'm not foolish enough to think that form of thinking is the best in every situation. It wouldn't be hard for me to imagine some scenarios where average people really struggled, where being average could be a liability.

Getting average and cutting corners while performing brain surgery probably isn't smart. Not sweating the small stuff is a bad idea for NASA engineers. Climbing Mount Everest on a whim is trouble. Being fun and fancy free while cave diving will get you killed.

There is a time to be perfect and a time to be special. But those perfect times are few and far between. You're better off keeping your eye on the big picture in most cases.

John Grace

Appendix Seven

(Just because)

A patient said to me one day, "We don't say it enough, probably? We don't tell you enough, maybe? But you know how wonderful you are, right?"

I answered sincerely. "Yes. I do."

I knew she wasn't talking about me being wonderful because I was smart. She was talking about me being wonderful because human beings are wonderful.

And I had convinced her that we're all wonderful. Average humans are wonderful.

Later that day my wife and I were walking down the street and an old couple passed. My wife looked and held my arm. "Isn't it sad, John? Nobody pays attention to them anymore. Nobody cares about old people. Nobody is nice to them or watches out for them.

Who is going take care of us John? Who is going to be nice to us? Who is going to listen to us? Aren't you scared?"

"No." I said.

"Why not? Who is going to be there for us?"

"Someone like me." I said. "I'd be nice to us when we get old."

She didn't understand why that gave me such comfort. My wife tends to think of me as something special. But now that I've given up on me being anything unique, I have a lot more faith in all of us because I know that if I care, and I'm average, then the rest of the world cares too.

If I *truly* believe in us, and I *truly* believe I'm average. Then I *know* we all believe.

John Grace

Appendix Eight

A special thank you to my wife for making this book, "Just so."

She has an innate ability to know the proper place of everything in the world and she has taught me that the right place for me is at her side.

Thank you Courtney. I LoVe **yOu!**

John Grace

Appendix Nine

A patient once said to me, "I checked your credentials on line. I had to make sure you were the best."

I smiled and said, "I'm not the best but why on earth would you think that *you* need the best? Most likely you have a pretty average problem."

John Grace

Appendix Ten

A lot of thank yous go into an average book. Here are some of mine. If I missed someone I'm sorry.

It gets easy to forget how many people help you in an average life.

But if I missed you and you want to be in here let me know.

I'll see what I can do.

Courtney, Amberly, Johnny, Dad and Mom and Bob. Jeanie and Laura, Mark and Sandy, Donna and Steve, Gloria and Shawn, Uncle Jerry and Michael, Theresa, and Mary. Uncle Paul, Nancy, Brian, Stephanie and Liz. Sandy and Fido. Uncle Johnny and Debbie. Matt, Kevin and Melissa. Flourtine and Annie. Jonda, Ed, Linda, Georgia, Dan, Grandpa and Grandma. Paw—paw. Mike, Beth and Mikey, Ben and Katie, Chris and Jerry. Rich, Dawn, Tony. Cindy and Steve. Joe and Carrissa. Virginia and Bill. Troy and Sherie. Darnell, Donna, Karen, Viola, and John, Ryan, Aileen, John, Maria, Christine, Ted, Scott, Alex, Bridget. Larry, Robyn, Tish and Doris. Janeth, Sheryl, Roz, Deb, Suzanne, Eric and Kathy, Diane, Patty, CNAs, Laura, Kristen. Mike, Cameron, Tom, Liz at McDonalds, Reyana John and Audrey, Fred, Perry, Tom, Lannie Glen, Curt, Neil, Laurie, Kallie, Tony, Jillian, Shannon, Mike, Cassie, Laura, Dr. H, Hap, Robert, Lucky, Jimmy, Mark, Jeff, Maureen, Rachel, Suzanne, John, Bill, Matt, Julko, Damian, Jennifer, Kenneth, John, Terrence, Dr. F. Vic, Aaron, Vern, Avi, Charlie, Todd, Mary Beth, Chris, Rachel, Adam, Voytek, Jeff, Brian, Paul, Sue, Terry, Jamie, Chris, Steve, Paul, Jerry, Sister M., Ms. R, Steve, Jason, Danna, Jeff, Brad, Jeff, Marty Scott, Pete, Cornelius, Beverly, Paul, Gene, Kaye, Kenneth, Steve, Jason, Granny, Grandma, Great Grandma.

John Grace

Appendix Eleven

Be Sure To Come Back

We've said again and again that the world doesn't make appreciating average easy. You'll probably feel better about average for the next few days, weeks, or even months. But then you'll slowly start to take your life too seriously. That's when it's time to come back and reread average.

You need to go through the process of feeling this book in order for it to have it's effect. The information conveyed in this book is simple but the emotional journey it describes is difficult.

Be sure to come back to keep you on the path of understanding yourself and appreciating your life. Every time you read this book, you'll get something different from it.

John Grace

Appendix Twelve

Average Afterlife?

If life is so fraught with mediocre and petty struggles, how could we possibly exist in Heaven? How are any of us going to exist in a perfect place?

No more waiting in line. No more bickering. No more worries, concerns. No more pain. Most of what we've thought of as our lives will be gone.

If my life and me are saturated with averageness, how much is going to be left when I enter, if I enter, the pearly gates?

My tardiness? My selfishness? My being confused easily? None of that stuff would make it. My bad parenting days? My average parenting days? None of those would make it in heaven.

My love for my little girl? Yeah. I guess that would make it. That's about as close to perfect as I ever know. I guess a place made up of that wouldn't be so bad.

Maybe little pieces of heaven slide into all of our days to help us make it through our average lives—maybe that little girl's smile was a glimpse of heaven bright enough to show me the way.

We have a name for the most average place in everyone's life. It's the place where most time passes and most of the time nothing special happens. It's a place we try to run from, but a place that we miss more than anything if we lose it. And we call that place—home.

Loving average means going home.

That's all I'm asking you to do.

John Grace

The Importance of Being Average

John Grace